NARROW

NOTES ON THE
BOOK OF RUTH

Discover How You Are Completely Accepted,
Deeply Loved, and Redeemed by God

BILL SPENCER

– NARROW GATE –

Copyright © 2022 Narrow Gate Foundation. All rights reserved.

Narrow Gate Foundation
P.O. Box 267
Duck River, TN 38454

All Scripture quotations are taken from the New King James Version®. Copyright © 1982 by Thomas Nelson. Used by permission. All rights reserved.

ISBN: 979-8-9868505-1-1

Printed in Canada

Table of Contents

Foreword		v
Introduction: Notes on the Book of Ruth		1
Chapter 1	**Far From Home**	6
Chapter 2	**The Field Of Boaz**	56
Chapter 3	**The Threshing Floor**	114
Chapter 4	**The City Gate**	156

Foreword

Why? I suppose that's a good question to begin with. Generations of theologians have written innumerable books containing invaluable insights into the mysteries of Scripture. Why would anyone want to pick up this little book? It's not the work of an accredited theologian who has spent a lifetime in the halls of academia gleaning wisdom and insight from heralded scholars. So, "Why" seems to be a fair question. Unfortunately, the answer isn't really all that remarkable.

For starters, thoughts move in and out of my head fast enough that if I don't write them down, I'll forget them (maybe you can relate). So, I take notes. To be fair, I rarely go back and *study* those notes. Sure, I refer to them from time to time, but I don't really *study* them, as if I'm preparing for an exam. I was always terrible at that sort of thing anyway. But I find that if I take notes and organize my thoughts while working through Scripture, the picture of my conversation with God becomes clearer. If I simply read and think, my mind drifts, and I rarely come to any clarified understanding that I can share with someone else. And isn't that the point of studying Scripture? To ingest something so deeply that its existence within you not only nourishes you but also gives you something to pass along to others?

The title of this book is fairly accurate. Not *The Mysteries Revealed* or *A Theological Commentary*. Instead, this is just a book of notes from one person who decided to write down what he saw as he studied his way through the text. But that still doesn't fully answer the question of why *you* are holding this book.

This book is far more than a record of *my notes* or *thoughts*. As you leaf through the pages, you'll notice that half of them are blank. The pages on the left contain pre-recorded notes, but the pages on the right have the heading "My Notes." These journal pages are the reasons why you're holding this book. Those pages are for you.

The notes contained in the book aren't designed to share insights that can't easily be found in multiple study resources. Rather, they are designed to get you to think and talk with God about His timeless and perfect expression of love toward you. The journal pages are designed adjacent to the populated ones so that you can record *your notes*. That's really the point of this exercise. It's not for you to learn what someone else thinks or knows; it's for you to record what you think and know. The notes are simply a primer for conversations between you and God. And that conversation is what truly matters.

As you record your thoughts, observations, insights, questions, and answers, you'll begin to connect more deeply with the text than you ever have before. And as you discover things for yourself, you'll have something to share with the people you encounter. That's the purpose of this book. You'll probably even notice, as you read through the pages that follow, that the recorded notes sound more like a discussion than observations. That's because I use my notes as a space where I can exercise how I'll share the insights of my study with the people I'll encounter. I'm not suggesting you should do the same, but it's a practice that has served me well for several years.

At Narrow Gate, where I spend the majority of my time, we're fond of saying, "Discovered Truth is always more powerful than delivered Truth." Here's your chance to discover Truth that you can carry in your soul and share with others for the rest of your life. Here's a chance for the words and thoughts of God to become *your* words and thoughts. When that happens, you'll begin to notice how the words of God migrate into your daily conversations. You'll find yourself discovering how the struggles of life from thousands of years in the past are still present with us today. You'll build a compass of unchanging Truth that will help you navigate the journey of our days from now until we see God face to face.

In short, if you'll take the time to compile Your Notes—your conversations with God about His timeless Truth—you'll be changed into a vessel of loving compassion that can be used to rescue and transform others. And that is a good answer to the question, "Why?"

So, let's get started.

Introduction
Notes on the Book of Ruth

I've lost track of how many people I've met who struggle with the question, "Am I really *loved* by God?" It manifests itself in a lot of ways: "Am I really saved?" "Can I really trust God for a good outcome?" "Is God mad at me?" "Am I being punished for past sins in my life? And if so, how long will this punishment last?" But the genesis of all those questions comes back to our original thought, "Does God really love me?"

I think there's probably a deeper thought that precipitates that question. It's a judgment that we typically pass on ourselves that winds up in contempt or condemnation for how we've fallen short in life. But do we ever stop to think about how God can juxtapose our view of self with His view of the redeemed self? Maybe an example would help.

Hebrews 11 begins by listing people who are named by God as examples of great faith. Noah, Abraham, and Sarah are just the beginning of the list. But if you compare the actions of their lives with the claim made by God, something doesn't add up. Genesis 9 records Noah being found in a naked and drunken stupor by his son. Genesis 18 records the fact that Sarah laughed at God in disbelief when He declared that she would have a child. That's not what I would call "great faith." Of course, Abraham was so riddled with doubt at God's ability to fulfill His promise of an offspring that Abraham took matters into his own hands (at the suggestion of Sarah, his wife) and fathered Ishmael through Sarah's handmaiden, Hagar. By all accounts, these individuals had every right to look at themselves and wonder whether God could actually love them and bless them despite their failings. Any one of them could have asked the question, "Does God really love me?"

The simple answer is, of course, yes!

It's an interesting exercise to scour the New Testament and see how the Old Testament patriarchs are discussed. To see how God still loved the patriarchs despite their shortcomings can be a deeply reassuring exercise for any believer. The event of the cross that separates the Old and New Testaments allows God to view us through the filter of forgiveness and redemption. "Their sins and their lawless deeds I will remember no more" is the promise (Hebrews 8:12). "As far as the east is from the west, so far has He removed our transgressions from us" (Psalm 103:12). When we arrive at the "hall of faith" listed in Hebrews 11, God has no obligation to remember the sins of Noah, Abraham, or Sarah. He sees them in light of Christ, and He is fully justified to love them and bless them as faithful followers and children of the King.

As we will review in the Book of Ruth, even Ruth suffered from the personal, earthly perspective that plagued her life. She addressed Boaz's kindness in chapter 2 by saying, "Why have I found favor in your eyes, that you should take notice of me?" (v. 10). Ruth couldn't see herself as Boaz saw her, so her doubt overshadowed the truth of his perspective.

If you can relate to this plight in the slightest way, the Book of Ruth is for you! I know of no other book in the Bible that (if properly read and rehearsed) can produce a truer sense of worth in the heart of a believer. I know of no other book in the Bible that establishes and reinforces the affectionate and sacrificial love that Jesus has toward His bride. I know of no book in the Bible that leaves the reader overwhelmed with a sense of God's loving perspective toward those that He has chosen to save. In short: If you want to feel the affectionate love of God, read the Book of Ruth!

The Book of Ruth is an incredibly short book. It's only four chapters long and can be read aloud in fourteen short minutes (I've done it more times than I can remember). I would strongly suggest that you begin your journey through this book by reading it in one sitting to either introduce the story to yourself or to refresh your memory regarding its plot. When you're finished, take a mental note of how you see the story and the impact it has on you. Then, begin to work your way through it.

When you've reached the end of this study, go back to the beginning and read the entire book in one sitting again. I think you'll find that your appreciation for the depth and beauty of the Book of Ruth will have changed dramatically. When you reach the end of that second reading, I would invite you to spend some time talking with Jesus about your newfound understanding of His affectionate, sacrificial, unwavering love for you. This exercise can rekindle your soul like no other I know. It's why I do it often. It's also why I introduce it to as many people as I possibly can.

May God bless your pursuit of Him with peace and joy as you find yourself in this story. And may God allow you to realize that you are loved, wanted, pursued, treasured, protected, fought for, drawn in, and given a secure and purposeful place in the arms of Jesus, our Bridegroom and Savior.

Who Wrote It?

The Book of Ruth was most probably written by Samuel, the prophet, although some commentators indicate that both Ezra and Hezekiah could have possibly written it. You'll remember Samuel as the man who stood for all that was holy and right in the midst of King Saul's failure to do what God had instructed him to do. If you need a refresher on that story, read 1 Samuel 15. God told Saul to rid the countryside of all Amalekites—including King Agag. When Saul failed to kill Agag, and instead took him captive, it was Samuel who called for Agag and "hacked Agag to pieces before the Lord in Gilgal" (v. 33). Samuel was committed to the dedicated work of God before he was conceived, and he fulfilled his station in life with excellence.

When Was It Written?

The Book of Ruth was probably composed during the earliest years of King David. Again, the actual date of penning is in question, but the most probable author and date have it being written by Samuel during the reign of King David. If our assumption is correct, the actual events of this book happened some 150 to 180 years prior to their recordation. The opening line tells us that the story takes place in the time of the Judges, and we can infer quite a lot about the timelines because people were interacting in peace. There is a website (actually it's a blog) called *pursiful.com* that contains some great, detailed information regarding this issue, and it makes a good, plausible argument for the fact that Ruth and Boaz began their courtship around 1131 BC, their son Obed was born in 1130 BC, and Jesse (Obed's son) was born in 1097 BC.

Why Was It Written?

The Book of Ruth appears to be written as a completion or "capstone" of First and Second Samuel. The story concludes with a lineage that clearly establishes David as the rightful King of Israel. Ruth and Boaz would have been David's great-grandparents. The book is read each year by the Jews during the Festival of Pentecost. The reason for its reading is fairly easy to understand: Exodus 23:16 prescribes an offering called "the first fruits of the harvest." This offering falls in conjunction with Pentecost, which celebrates the giving of the Law on Mt. Sinai. Ruth and Boaz's courtship would have happened during this time period—when the first fruits of the wheat harvest were being gleaned.

From the viewpoint of the modern church, the book plays a very different role. It is one of the most symbolic books in all of Scripture, and it tells the story of Christ and His Church. It is a great piece of literature that displays how all things in the Old Testament point to Jesus, and it gives us a tangible picture of the mercy and character that Christ demonstrated by making us (the Church) His Bride.

Many of us have heard the phrase, "The New Testament is in the Old Testament, concealed." I cannot think of any writing that better demonstrates this point than the Book of Ruth. When you need to introduce someone to the importance of the Old Testament text or the Truth of Christ's revelation in the words of the Jews, just turn to Ruth and walk them through the symbolism. You'll both be amazed at the lengths God went to in order to show the undeniable passion He has for the salvation of man.

Why Should We Read It?

This one is simple: It's difficult to get your head and heart wrapped around the idea that a "perfect and righteous God thinks that I am beautiful, desirable, and worth sacrificing for." It's much easier to believe that "He simply puts up with me and displays love toward me because it's His obligatory nature to do so." But the Book of Ruth paints the perfect picture of a Savior beyond our reach who gets one glimpse of us and immediately sets His heart on winning us for Himself. If you have ever wanted to feel the affectionate love of God directed toward you—in your broken and undeserving state—Ruth is the book for you.

Okay, let's get started.

CHAPTER 1

Far From Home

> **1:1-2** | "Now it came to pass, in the days when the judges ruled, that there was a famine in the land. And a certain man of Bethlehem, Judah, went to dwell in the country of Moab, he and his wife and his two sons. The name of the man *was* Elimelech, the name of his wife *was* Naomi, and the names of his two sons *were* Mahlon and Chilion—Ephrathites of Bethlehem, Judah. And they went to the country of Moab and remained there."

We can't even get out of the first verse of this book without falling straight into the symbolism of its contents. The backdrop is set, and then the symbolism begins. Let's start with the backdrop:

Samuel begins by telling us that these things transpired ("it came to pass") in the time of the Judges. So, what do we know about the time of the Judges? If you've ever read the Book of Judges, you probably found it to be one of the most frustrating series of stories you've ever laid eyes on. A people (the Hebrews) had been delivered from slavery and brought to a fertile and lush countryside through the sovereign protection of God Almighty. They were given the land and protected, despite their repeated unwillingness to do things the way God had

MY NOTES

instructed them. If we dove into the Book of Judges, we would find that God had established a government of judges to guide the wellbeing of His beloved people—but they consistently did whatever they wanted rather than listening to the direction of God. The ethic of the day is represented well in Judges 17:6 and repeated as the concluding thought in Judges 21:25: "In those days there was no king in the land. Everyone did what was right in his own eyes."

Repeatedly, their behavior gets them in hot water with the neighbors that they were supposed to have driven out of the land in the first place. Things get tough, and they cry out to God. Things get better, and they go back to doing whatever they want. Things get tough—God rescues. Things get good—they get selfish. The rollercoaster effect leaves the reader wanting to yell at the people in the text, "For goodness sake! When will you ever learn?" But then again, I want to yell that at myself fairly often.

This is the backdrop that frames our story and it's not a pretty setting. It's a bleak picture of man at the height of sinfulness. The children of God were living in such a way that it can easily be compared to our mindset today: live according to our own desires, until those desires take us into a place of difficulty, conflict, oppression, or danger. Then we cry out to God, "Save me!" The amazing thing about the Book of Judges is that God does what the people cry out for: He saves them, knowing that they are only going to return to their independence again and again.

The second sentence of verse one states that there was a famine in the land. Jewish tradition surrounding the Targum Onkelos (one of the circulated translations of the Hebrew TORH translated into Aramaic) holds that God had decreed ten famines to occur before the coming

MY NOTES

of Christ the King. One of those famines was to occur in the time of "Ibzan the just, of Bethlehem Judah." This is that famine. These famines may have been caused by the Ammonites or other Canaanite clans performing raids on the Israelite crops. The amazing thing about the famines is that God always delivered the Hebrews from them if the people remained faithful—or even if they didn't, for that matter. God also declared in Leviticus 26:19 that a famine would be the method He would use to break the prideful spirit of the Hebrew people when they began to live independently from Him in the promised land. In any case, this is one of those times when you wish that the Hebrews would look back on their history and see that the time of famine was temporary and that the answer was always found by turning to God, and not by taking matters into their own hands. Nevertheless, we see them doing exactly that—taking matters into their own hands and heading for greener pastures.

So, let's begin dissecting the symbolism.

In verse two, we see that there was a certain man who lived in Bethlehem, Judah. As you may know, Judah was in the southern section of the promised land, and Bethlehem was a small town just south of Jerusalem. If you recall the story of the Magi who traveled to see Jesus at His birth, you'll remember them following a star that led them to Jerusalem and then south to Bethlehem (Matthew 2:1-12). In our story, we see a man who lived in this little village pulling up stakes and heading off to another location in search of a better life. Not only did he go, but he also took his whole family.

Let's use some rationale here and see if what we are reading makes sense. There is a guy who has a wife and two kids, and a famine strikes the land where he lives. He, being a good and responsible husband and

MY NOTES

father, takes his family and moves to a new town in hopes of finding the proverbial "greener pasture." To me, that makes good sense. This guy is being responsible and has a good, defensible rationale for why he made his choice; it was for the good of his family—right?

Well, let's consider the towns in question. First, Bethlehem means "house of bread," and Judah means "place of praise." Now that sounds like a great place to live. Furthermore, he moves his family to a place called Moab. In both Psalm 60 and Psalm 108, God declares, "Moab *is* My wash pot" (v. 9). That's a "nice" way to translate what is being said here because a wash pot is merely a toilet bowl. Moab (the man) was the oldest son of Lot (Abraham's brother-in-law) by an incestuous relationship. So, this guy in the opening of our story (Elimelech) moves from the "house of bread" in the "place of praise" to the "toilet bowl." (This is the point where we all giggle and talk about what a stupid decision this is. But let's hold the laughter until we've done some real self-analysis.)

The circumstances in which Elimelech found himself back home were difficult—but that's because God always sent famine as a judgment of man's disobedience. Remember, we already discussed what God said about famine in Leviticus (and other places). "Correction" is always designed to cause change (Leviticus 26:19-20). "Punishment," on the other hand, is a cost exacted for an evil decision. But the measures that are present in the opening of our story were designed as a correction to cause the Hebrew people to repent. God caused hardship so that His people would cry out and return to Him. The right decision for Elimelech (which, by the way, his name means "my God; my King" or "God is my King") would have been for him to hit his knees in prayer and cry out to God, "Lord, save me and my family!"

MY NOTES

So, what about us? How many times have we rebelled against God only to have correction sent our way and then respond by finding a way to fix the situation? We think that the situation is the problem when, almost always, the situation is nothing more than an "attention-getter." God is anxiously awaiting our return to total dependence on Him. But far too often, we do not turn to Him for our solution. We take matters into our own hands and make decisions like Elimelech's: "I'll run from the 'house of bread' and the 'place of praise' because the solution to my problem is waiting for me in the 'toilet bowl' of life." In short, we look at difficulty as something to be "fixed" or "solved," instead of an orchestrated opportunity to turn to God and cry out for help from a loving Father who always and only wants what's best for His children. Find yourself in Elimelech and learn a lesson!

> **1:3** | "Then Elimelech, Naomi's husband, died; and she was left, and her two sons."

It's worth noting that "Naomi" means "pleasant." So, if you read the meanings of the names and places, you can construct an opening line to our story that would sound like this, *"There once was a man whose very name declared that God was his King. He lived in a 'house of bread' nestled into the 'place of praise' and was given a wife whose essence was exemplified in her name—pleasant."*

If we don't take a brief moment to consider the opening lines of the story, we miss a critical component of context that reminds us of a timeless and immovable Truth. Our ultimate position in life is often obscured by our immediate circumstances. Sometimes looking beyond the immediate circumstances to remember the ultimate Truth is the key to living *through* the circumstances with joy, peace, patience, kindness, goodness,

MY NOTES

faithfulness, gentleness, and self-control (see Galatians 5:22-23). It's amazing what we subject ourselves to when we forsake God's design for our lives—or when we follow those who do. When this family followed the un-Godly direction of a man who was forsaking the design of his Maker, the whole family would pay the price. By the way, the two kids, Mahlon and Chilion, their names mean "sickness" and "consumption." I'll leave that one for you to contemplate. Let's just call it sufficient to say that the pursuit of the things of this world (as a means of fulfillment) will consistently take its toll on us and those we love.

> **1:4** | "Now they took wives of the women of Moab: the name of the one *was* Orpah, and the name of the other Ruth. And they dwelt there about ten years."

When the Hebrew people moved into the land of Canaan (Israel), they were instructed to drive out every inhabitant of the land. One of the reasons for that instruction was because God knew that eventually, the Hebrews would begin to marry the foreigners and those spouses would bring their pagan worship into the family of God. Ezra and Nehemiah both railed against this practice later. So what do we see here? Since Elimelech made the decision to remove his family from the company of God's people, his sons married women of the world. Please let this be a lesson for us when we have sons and daughters of our own. Removing our families from the company of God's people will expose them to the "attractive" things of the world. That fact runs far beyond "who they marry." The Church (God's people) is designed to be the environment where we learn what it means to be a disciple of Jesus in our family, our work, our recreation, and our internal relationship with God.

MY NOTES

One other observation here: Evidently the people of God (Elimelech's family) got really comfortable in the world; they stayed there for ten years after his death, and it appears that they had no intention of leaving. However, God used circumstances, once again, to guide this family into the place where He needed them to be. That process begins in the story as the boys take wives and their father passes away. The next verse thickens the plot a bit.

> **1:5 |** "Then both Mahlon and Chilion also died; so the woman survived her two sons and her husband."

Well, we are only five verses into this story, and it's already full of action. The way Scripture is composed always intrigues me. Reading these five verses is much like reading the story found in Luke 15 of the father who had two sons. So few words are used to say so much that we could stop right here and realize a rather lengthy life-lesson out of what we've read. It appears that Naomi's willingness to act contrary to the design of God's plan for her life has left her in a very difficult position. She, like her husband before her, had her reasons for following Elimelech into Moab. But now she's having to face the outcome of her former rationale. The circumstances she's facing are a direct result of the choices she and her husband made a decade earlier. It's kind of brutal to say it this way, but she has no one to blame but herself for the tough spot she's in. And now she's paying the price.

Let's address something before we go any farther. In this life we will have problems! Jesus declared this, not me (John 16:33). If Elimelech and Naomi had chosen to stay in Bethlehem, Judah, they would have faced the drought. They ran to avoid that hardship. But now Naomi finds herself in an even more difficult set of circumstances. Understanding

MY NOTES

this truth goes a long way in teaching us how to respond to the fact that we will face difficulty in this life. Embracing the struggle allows us to turn to Christ, who joined (and continues to join) us in our struggles. God does not bring about difficulty to drive us away. He brings about difficulty to turn us back to Himself and refine the character of Jesus in our lives. This truth is shown in the next verse when our story takes an abrupt turn.

> **1:6 |** "Then she arose with her daughters-in-law that she might return from the country of Moab, for she had heard in the country of Moab that the LORD had visited His people by giving them bread."

It seems that God kept His promise: He gave bread to the "house of bread." Naomi found that her venture into the world provided some temporary satisfaction, but it had ended empty and hollow. Her husband and her sons were dead, and at this point in our story, she was left with two daughters-in-law that aren't even Hebrews. She was alone in a foreign land. And when she finally came face-to-face with the result of her choices, she thought of home. Doesn't that sound a lot like the story of the younger son (the Prodigal) in Luke 15?

> **1:7 |** "Therefore she went out from the place where she was, and her two daughters-in-law with her; and they went on the way to return to the land of Judah."

Just a quick thought here: These two girls, Orpah and Ruth, were in a similar predicament as their mother-in-law. They had, at least in part, left their native culture and joined in marriage to a foreign one.

MY NOTES

Their husbands (their principal attachment to the foreign culture) had died. And the only remaining tie to the marital/cultural commitment they had made was leaving town. They were at a crossroads, forced to choose between two distinct lives. We'll say more about this later, but we need to read the next section before we have a discussion about the symbolism being written into our story. Let's read on.

> **1:7-13** | "And Naomi said to her two daughters-in-law, 'Go, return each to her mother's house. The LORD deal kindly with you, as you have dealt with the dead and with me. The LORD grant that you may find rest, each in the house of her husband.' So she kissed them, and they lifted up their voices and wept. And they said to her, 'Surely we will return with you to your people.' But Naomi said, 'Turn back, my daughters; why will you go with me? *Are* there still sons in my womb, that they may be your husbands? Turn back, my daughters, go—for I am too old to have a husband. If I should say I have hope, *if* I should have a husband tonight and should also bear sons, would you wait for them till they were grown? Would you restrain yourselves from having husbands? No, my daughters; for it grieves me very much for your sakes that the hand of the LORD has gone out against me!'"

If you're reading this text with a western perspective, this is some fairly strange conversation going on here. It reads like Naomi is suggesting that one alternative for Orpah and Ruth would be for her (Naomi) to re-marry and have two more sons. Then once those babies grew up to be adult men, they could serve as "replacement husbands" for Mahlon

and Chilion. Even Naomi is expressing that she thought this was a terrible idea.

But in order to more fully grasp what's going on, we'll need to understand an aspect of Hebrew law regarding family. In Deuteronomy 25:5-10, there is a practice established called Levirate Law or Levirate Marriage. This is how it worked: If a man took a wife and she did not bear him a son and the man then died, the man's closest relative (usually a brother) took that wife in marriage. Then that couple would try to have a child to fulfill the Levirate Law. If they succeeded, their firstborn son would carry the name of the deceased husband. It's as if the child's father was actually the deceased husband. This process ensured that the name of the deceased man would not pass from the lineage of the Hebrews. That means that the child (son) would inherit everything that belonged to his deceased father, and he would be allowed to sit in his father's position at the city gate. The closest relative who performed this act was called the "GO'EL" or "kinsman-redeemer." (We'll talk a lot more about this as the book unfolds.) However, the closest relative could refuse the woman if he chooses to. The only problem with refusing the widow was that it came with a great deal of shame. Read the above-referenced passage in Deuteronomy to get a full picture of the process and you'll see that it involved public humiliation in a terrible way (if you were a Jewish man).

Now with that in mind, let's take a look at the conversation and decisions made in these six verses. We begin with Naomi, who made a very difficult decision. As an old woman with two young daughters-in-law, she recognized something that was presented very subtly in the text. In verses 6, 7, 8, and 9, she mentioned "The LORD" in three of the four verses. Naomi was a very broken woman; her life had been difficult, and

MY NOTES

she was facing the end of her life reaping the consequences of decisions made well over a decade earlier. However, in her despair she considered the goodness of God and how He had re-visited the land of Bethlehem. She recognized her rightful place, and she exercised repentance by declaring that she would return to the place where she belonged. She had given up the practice of manipulating circumstances for gain and was committing her life to the care of God—as she should.

Next, she offered a farewell to her daughters-in-law by blessing them in the name of the Lord. She addressed the fact that they had dealt kindly with her and her family and she wished them two things. First, that they may be taken back in by their people. Remember that these women had married foreigners, and had, to some degree, forsaken their own culture. Now it was Naomi's desire that these women be accepted back into their mother's homes, despite their former choice to abandon them.

Second, she wished for them to have new husbands. The greatest honor for a woman of this time period was to bear children. A husband is a necessary element for this glory to be achieved, and Naomi was aware of the fact that these are young women who had much of their adult lives still ahead of them.

Verse 10 shows just how kind the women actually were: "Surely we will return with you to your people." They were looking at an old woman potentially going to her demise, and they didn't have the heart to say, "Okay, see you later. Have a nice rest of your life."

This, of course, brings Naomi to make her forward-thinking argument. In a sense, she says, "Girls, be rational. You know our culture of Levirate Marriage, but what do you think is going to happen? Do you think I am going to marry again? I'm old! Besides, even if I did marry,

MY NOTES

I'm too old to bear children. And even if by some miracle I could bear sons, would you wait for them to grow into young men so that you could marry them and have children. You would be old before you even got the opportunity. This plan of you staying with me is crazy. Go and have a life."

Then she makes her final reference to "The Lord," saying, "The hand of the Lord has gone out against me!" I love this moment. Naomi realized that she was suffering the consequences of her decisions. She didn't blame her husband for leading her to a place where she didn't want to be. She owns the fact that she had a role in the way things had worked out. Yet, she was returning to the very Lord whose "hand is against her." After opening our story with a husband who doesn't get the corrective mechanism of God, we quickly get to a wife who understood the ways of God and walked in humble obedience and trust. I like the way this section ends! And I pray that God will make me more like Naomi in the moments where I am forced to come fact-to-face with my poor choices.

As we move on, it's imperative to know that the Levirate Marriage theme is *huge* in this book. The author has foreshadowed the ending of the story for us! So, don't forget this whole concept. We'll see it come full circle soon enough.

A Tough Decision

> **1:14 |** "Then they lifted up their voices and wept again; and Orpah kissed her mother-in-law, but Ruth clung to her."

Now the true colors begin to come out; we see two different responses in this moment. These women are hugging and crying.

MY NOTES

Naomi's mind and heart was set on returning to Bethlehem, and the girls have been freed to return to their culture, families, and lives. Then, Orpah kissed Naomi. She showed affection and fondness. But ultimately her desire for what *she* wanted wins out. She listened to Naomi's argument and agreed with it. She saw that the 'logical' pathway to happiness in life was not going to be found in joining Naomi on this journey back to Israel. In truth the decision she made is very similar to the decisions made in the opening of this book. She weighed the circumstances and took matters into her own hands—rather than depending on the God she had come to know though her time with this Jewish family.

Ruth, on the other hand, clung to Naomi. Her desire was for commitment in love. She saw the trust that Naomi was putting in the Lord and she vowed to make that trust her own. We know that because of the next three verses. But before we read on, these two choices should teach us something about our own lives. There's an adage that says, "Most lessons are more caught than taught." If we would make intentional decisions to *display* our trust in God more than *talk* about it, we could stop worrying about always having the right words. We could actually trust God to win the hearts of *those who will*, and we could be free to love everyone without taking on responsibilities that don't belong to us. Think of it this way: "Our job: love people. God's job: change people."

Okay; let's look at those next three verses.

> **1:15-17 |** "And she said, 'Look, your sister-in-law has gone back to her people and to her gods; return after your sister-in-law.' But Ruth said: 'Entreat me not to leave you, *Or to* turn back from following after you; For wherever you go, I will go;

MY NOTES

> And wherever you lodge, I will lodge; Your people *shall be* my people, And your God, my God. Where you die, I will die, And there will I be buried. The LORD do so to me, and more also, If *anything but* death parts you and me.'"

    This world will always be filled with folks who have a fondness for Jesus or the things of God. Orpah was such a person. She showed affection for Naomi and even began a journey into the family of God. However, when the offer to pursue an easier course was presented, she turned from her original fondness to serve her own best interest. The most telling line in this verse is that Orpah returned not only to her people but "to her gods" as well. This is just one more reiteration of the fact that we are heavily influenced by the people with whom we associate. Elimelech's mistake was to leave the family of God and subject both himself and his family to the things of this world. Now we see Orpah making the same choice. She has the opportunity to travel with Naomi and keep her affiliation with the true and living God. However, when she counts the cost of that decision, she is like the man in Matthew 19, who was told to sell all he had and give it to the poor and then come and follow Jesus. Scripture tells us that the man went away sad. Even Jesus's disciples were "greatly astonished" and said, "Who then can be saved?" That's when Jesus said that "With men this is impossible, but with God all things are possible" (Matthew 19:25-26). Remember, when you are facing a seemingly impossible decision, God can do the impossible *for* you and *through* you.

    Turning back to Ruth, we see a completely different picture. Here was a woman who knew the cost as well as her sister-in-law. And, yet, she saw something that Orpah did not. She recognized the commitment

MY NOTES

in Naomi to her God. She heard the acknowledgement of Naomi's repentant faith toward God, even though God had dealt harshly with her. Ruth, recognizing her own commitment of marriage, vowed to stay by Naomi's side—even if it meant she would suffer the same harsh consequences or worse.

The real line to grab in this reference from Ruth was, "Your people will be my people and your God will be my God." This foreshadowing is staggering. Ruth was declaring that her decision to follow Naomi was based in a belief that this true and living God of the Hebrews would ultimately reward her kindness and dedication—and she was right. In a broader sense, this is a foreshadowing statement regarding all Gentile peoples and all the Jews. With the introduction of Jesus, the Jewish people truly are our people, and the Jewish God truly is our God.

> **1:18** | "When she saw that she was determined to go with her, she stopped speaking to her."

Sometimes the most effective thing you can do when someone makes a decision to chase after God is to shut up and get out of the way. Naomi saw that there was no need in challenging Ruth's decision further. Besides, I have to wonder if she didn't secretly want Ruth and Orpah to go with her, and she was just doing the noble act by offering a way to escape. We'll never know all that went through Naomi's mind; the text doesn't afford us that insight. But this is the turning point of the story: The people of God (Elimelech and family) had ventured out into the world (much like the prodigal); they paid a terrible price (much like the prodigal); and now they were returning home (much like the prodigal) with the *world* in tow.

MY NOTES

> **1:19** | "Now the two of them went until they came to Bethlehem. And it happened, when they had come to Bethlehem, that all the city was excited because of them; and the women said, '*Is this Naomi?*'"

The ravages of the world can leave you almost unrecognizable. Nevertheless, the only proper way for the people of God to respond when one of their own returned home was to be unanimously excited. Remember the ecstasy of the father in Luke 15 when he saw his son returning? If so, you'll also remember the completely inappropriate attitude of the older brother as the younger son was celebrated. It's a sad commentary that people avoid church because they believe that they simply cannot be loved and welcomed *as they are*. If we could start welcoming the world into our midst *as they are*, we might be shocked to see how many of them would get a glimpse of *who they are* in the sight of God for the first time. It's worth considering.

> **1:20-21** | "But she said to them, 'Do not call me Naomi; call me Mara, for the Almighty has dealt very bitterly with me. I went out full, and the LORD has brought me home again empty. Why do you call me Naomi, since the LORD has testified against me, and the Almighty has afflicted me?"

This leg of the journey for Naomi is now complete. Naomi said that when she left this "house of bread" in "the place of praise" she had everything—she was full. If you had asked her on the day she left, she would have told you how hard things were in the famine. Isn't that our way—to focus on what we are missing or how difficult our circumstances?

MY NOTES

I can tell you from experience that often times God will have to take you to a much more difficult place in order to enable you to see just how good life really was in your day of complaint. Now—years later—Naomi looked back on her life in Bethlehem, and she declared that she had it all. She said that she went out "full" and had returned "empty." So, the next time you want to feel a little sorry for yourself and your current difficulties just shift your focus. Ask yourself what you have to celebrate and then begin to list the answers. It's a lot like the guy who arrived at the grocery store and the only parking spot was a quarter-mile from the front door. He grumbled all the way to the entrance about the inconvenience of the walk. The friendly greeter inside the grocery store was a young lady in a wheelchair who was born without legs. Perspective.

Finally, Naomi was so despondent over her mistakes in life that she refused her name. She asked that no one refer to her as pleasant any longer because that name represented a life that *used* to be hers through the grace of God. She now requested that people address her in accordance with the way God had dealt with her. She asked to be called "Mara," which means bitter. You may read this as a complaint, but I don't. I see Naomi honestly, humbly, and transparently admitting her station in life. Isn't it wonderful that it is from this position that God will restore her greatest desires?

> **1:22 |** "So Naomi returned, and Ruth the Moabitess her daughter-in-law with her, who returned from the country of Moab. Now they came to Bethlehem at the beginning of barley harvest."

Naomi and Ruth arrive at Bethlehem as the priests of Judaism are making the offering of the "first fruits" during the seasons of Passover

MY NOTES

and Pentecost. (Don't worry if you don't know what that means; we're going to discuss it.) This arrival is perfectly timed to give us a picture of Jew *and* Gentile coming into new life through the process of law, sin, repentance, and grace. However, the picture is subtle, so we'll need to know some things about the way the offerings of first fruits were made during the seasons of Passover and Pentecost.

Remember that when we were introducing this book, I mentioned that the Jews read this story every year at the Feast of Pentecost. That's because the large majority of this story took place at the time of Pentecost. It's a vital part of the Jewish history and, more specifically, that of King David. There is a lot of information that comes together in conjunction with this harvest time, so I'm going to try and break things down in components. It may seem like these things are a bit disconnected at first, but if we see this exercise through to the end, the symbolism of this book will become truly astounding.

Passover and the Barley Harvest: The offering of the first fruits included both of the grain crops that were gathered in the spring. Winter had given way to crops planted in the months before, and winter barley and wheat were harvested in the spring. The barley harvest happened at the same time that the Jews were celebrating Passover. It is said that the Jews went into Egypt a family (the family of "Jacob" who became "Israel") and came out a nation. So, arguably, the Jewish nation began its birth process as it was freed from Egypt's bonds. Passover commemorates the freedom that came to the Jews when the angel of the Lord "passed over" each home that had the blood of a spotless lamb applied to its doorposts, threshold, and lintel. By the way, if you connect the points where the blood was applied to the doorway, you get the figure of a cross. Basin (threshold) to lintel is bottom to top and doorpost

MY NOTES

to doorpost is left to right. The Jews gather in Jerusalem annually on the Sabbath of Nissan 14 (Nissan is a month in the Jewish lunar calendar) to celebrate this miraculous night. On Friday night, as the sun sets and three stars appear to begin the Sabbath, they re-create the meal that was shared in captivity and re-tell the story of their liberation. They continue the celebration on Saturday (and the whole following week) by abstaining from eating anything that has leaven (yeast) in it. A study of Exodus 12 will help explain why they don't eat leavened bread during this holy celebration. Finally, on Sunday, which is the *first* day of the week, they celebrate with an offering of the first fruits (the first barley they collect from the fields) as a show of gratitude for God's sustaining provision. So, we begin our picture of Jewish tradition by recognizing that the offering of the first fruits began in conjunction with the celebration of Passover. These are the Spring Feasts: Passover, Unleavened Bread, First Fruits.

Pentecost and the Wheat Harvest: The offering of the first fruits continued with the second great harvest of spring/summer. Wheat was gathered at the time of Pentecost, which is fifty days after the Passover. Pentecost marks the day when Moses came down from Mt. Sinai with the stone tablets of Law from God. If the delivery of the Jews from Egypt marks the beginning of the birth of a nation, the giving of the Law marks the completion of that birth. With the Law, the Hebrew people became a nation unto themselves. And although another forty years would pass before they inherited the land that would be their home, Pentecost is the birthday of Judaism. This happened a couple hundred years before the events of the Book of Ruth, so the practices of celebrating the offering of first fruits at Passover and Pentecost had been well established.

Celebrating the Offering of First Fruits During Pentecost: Pentecost included a very *strange* practice, which is thoroughly detailed

MY NOTES

in Leviticus 23. (As a matter of fact, a *thorough* study of the seven feasts listed in Leviticus 23 would be a great companion to the study of Ruth. But that's another book of notes for another time.) This chapter of Leviticus mandates that a "wave" offering (waving loaves of bread before God as to *offer* them to Him) be made for the Passover in conjunction with the Barley Harvest, and then it instructs for a new grain offering to be made at the Feast of Pentecost (sometimes called the Feast of Weeks). The odd thing about this second wave offering is that it is the only time the Jews are instructed to have leaven in the bread (see Leviticus 23:17).

The reason I say it's a bit strange is that God goes out of His way in Leviticus 2:11 to command the Jews to *never* offer bread with leaven. But on this occasion, He specifically instructs that the bread offered *should* be leavened. We know that leaven is a *type* for sin in Scripture—meaning that any time you see leaven mentioned it represents sin. Types are used in the Bible to represent or prefigure deeper spiritual truths. That is why God is so adamant about getting rid of all leaven in the Jews' offering. Jews thoroughly clean their homes at Passover because any trace of "chametz" (yeast or leaven) is an affront to God. As a matter of fact, Jews aren't even legally allowed to own chametz or have it in their possession during the Passover. As an aside, this process of ridding the home of chametz is rumored by some to be where the tradition of "spring cleaning" came from. Parents would intentionally sprinkle the crumbs of bread and cookies in the house and allow the children to spend the day finding and ridding the home of those crumbs. The final product was a very clean home.

The command to make a wave offering to God at the Feast of Pentecost is very specific. Scripture tells us that the High Priest is to

MY NOTES

wave two loaves of leavened bread before God. Now, if you ask a Jew why they wave the two loaves of bread at Pentecost, they will tell you it is because those two loaves represent the two tablets of Law that were brought down by Moses at Mt. Sinai. Remember, Pentecost is the birthday of Judaism when the Law was given to a family to be governed as a nation. So then you need to ask why the leaven is left in the bread. If the loaves represent the Law, are they saying that the Law contains sin? They will answer, "Certainly not," as Paul does in Romans 7:7 when he asks that very question (*Is* the Law sin?). So this leaves us with an unanswered question in this strange Jewish tradition: "Why is the leaven in the bread?" Hold on to that thought for a minute while we take a short diversion.

Naomi and Ruth show up at the beginning of the barley harvest, which means it is Passover time. But the "season" of the offering of the first fruits lasts through Passover and extends into Pentecost. And this story takes place as the whole season unfolds. We'll see later that Ruth stayed close to the maidservants of Boaz throughout the *barley* harvest *and* the *wheat* harvest.

We need to table our discussion of Jewish traditions for a moment and think about this season in a different light—a Christian light. As you probably know, the Jewish celebration of Passover is paralleled by the Christian celebration of Easter: Jesus was crucified just before the Sabbath of Passover, and He rose on the first day of that week. His last supper with His disciples was actually a Passover celebration (see Matthew 26:17). In the same way that the beginning of Passover kicked off the offering of the first fruits, Jesus's death (because He is the ultimate Passover Lamb) was the offering that brought about the first fruits of life, as Jesus became the "*first born* among many brethren" (Romans 8:29).

MY NOTES

Next, Pentecost was in full swing when the Holy Spirit of God descended on the multitude gathered when Peter preached the first gospel sermon in Acts 2. That day marks the birth of the Church as we know it today. So, just as the Jews celebrated the Passover and Pentecost, we celebrate Easter and Pentecost. Passover and Easter both represent the sparing of life through the sacrifice of death. Pentecost represents the birthday of Judaism as the Law was given, and it also represents the birthday of the Church as the Holy Spirit was given.

With that in mind, we need to re-visit our unresolved question regarding the "leaven in the loaves" that were offered as a wave offering during Pentecost. The wording that surrounds this offering is very unique in Levitical Law. It says, "It shall be a statute forever in all your generations" (Leviticus 6:18). This statement is only made in conjunction with the grain offerings.

As we look at the wave offering (a grain offering), we see this one offering on the Day of Pentecost where the Jews are instructed to have leaven in their bread. The Jews say that the two loaves of bread represent the Law but we know that leaven is a type for sin. So, this must be an incomplete answer. However, let's draw one parallel from their thinking. On the day that the Law was given and Moses descended from the mountain, in what situation did he find the children of Israel? They were naked and dancing around a golden calf—an idol (see Exodus 32:19). He found them in sin. Next, we need to ask what the result of that circumstance was. Because of the sin of the people in the presence of the Law, 3,000 people died on that day. Drawing from this account, we can see that the presence of the Law and the presence of sin go hand-in-hand.

Paul spends several chapters in Romans explaining that the Law makes us aware of sin and that sin can only bring death. However, he

MY NOTES

goes on to say that the Holy Spirit brings life. So let's look at a different story. We've already addressed the fact that Pentecost is the birthday of Judaism (under the Law) and the Church (under the Holy Spirit). If we look at the circumstances surrounding Pentecost as the birth of the Church, what do we find? We see sinful people gathered together to hear a message of hope. The Holy Spirit is poured out and the Church is born. In the same way that 3,000 people died when Moses introduced the law, 3,000 people were saved on the day that the Holy Spirit gave birth to the Church.

I would propose this: As Jews wave the two loaves of bread before the alter of God, they hold two representations of the people of God; the Jews and the Christians share a day of birth. Paul says in Ephesians 2:15-16, "having abolished in His flesh the enmity, *that is,* the Law of commandments *contained* in ordinances, so as to create in Himself one new man from the two, *thus* making peace, and that He might reconcile them both to God in one body through the cross, thereby putting to death the enmity." I would propose that the two loaves of bread represent the two men (Jew and Gentile)—both sinful—being made one in the newness of life through the finished work of God in Christ. After all, those two loaves of bread that contain the type for sin are in the hands of the High Priest. And isn't it our High Priest who presents us to God as righteous because we are in Him?

This sheds great light on the symbolism of the Book of Ruth because it tells of a Gentile woman being brought into the family of God through the action of a kinsman-redeemer (as we'll see in the chapters ahead). How appropriate it is that this story unfolds as the Priests appear before the altar of God to wave their leavened loaves to the God who would make provision to rescue both!

MY NOTES

Review: Chapter 1

I was once told that *Bible reading* is the process of allowing God to speak to you, and *Bible study* is the process of allowing God to prepare you so that He can speak through you to others. The questions that follow are designed to prepare us to have a conversation with other people about the text of Ruth, and how it still has practical implication for our lives today. Knowing some basic background facts about the book can add credibility to our insights. In short, people are more inclined to believe what we say if our conversation reveals that we've done our homework! Knowing how the deeper truths of the story serve as a commentary about the call to love God and love others can prepare us to offer eternal, loving hope to anyone we choose to share those truths with.

1. If you were asked, who would you say wrote the Book of Ruth? When? Why? _____

   _____

2. At what point in the Jewish calendar was this book read aloud annually? _____

3. Why did Elimelech move his family from their homeland?

   _____

   _____

RUTH 1 REVIEW

4. Where did Elimelech move his family to? What did God say about that region? Where does God say it? _____

   _____

5. What are the literal translations of the following names?

   a. Elimelech: _____

   b. Naomi: _____

   c. Mara: _____

   d. Mahlon: _____

   e. Chilion: _____

   f. Bethlehem: _____

   g. Judah: _____

6. Using the translations above, what lesson can we derive from the introduction of our characters in Ruth, chapter 1?

   _____

   _____

   _____

7. What are the names of the wives of Mahlon and Chilion?

   _____ and _____

8. Explain why, in Ruth 1:12-13, Naomi asked the question, "If I were to have sons, would you wait for them till they are grown?"

   _____

   _____

9. What are the differences between Orpah's response to Naomi's offer and Ruth's response? _____
   _____

10. What lesson do we derive from the responses in question 9 regarding how people respond to Jesus? _____
    _____
    _____

11. What is the significance of the second half of verse 18, which reads, "Your people shall be my people and your God, my God"?
    _____
    _____

12. The story of Ruth stretched from the Barley Harvest to the Wheat Harvest. What two major feasts accompany those two harvests? _____ and _____

13. Pentecost (Wheat Harvest) represents the birthday of Judaism. What event happened to give birth to Judaism that is celebrated on Pentecost? What was the result on that day? _____
    _____
    _____

14. Pentecost (Wheat Harvest) represents the birthday of Christianity. What event happened to give birth to Christianity on Pentecost? What was the result on that day? _____
    _____
    _____

15. In Leviticus 2, God instructed the Jews to never offer a grain offering that contains _____.

16. In Leviticus 23:17, God instructed the High Priest to make a specific offering during Pentecost. How does that offering seemingly contradict an earlier command (see question 15) and why is that important? _____

_____

_____

17. In the space that follows, describe the Pentecost offering of Leviticus 23, and explain how Jews justify the instruction as opposed to how Christians understand the significance of the Pentecost offering. _____

_____

_____

_____

18. How would you summarize the happenings, insights, and lessons you are taking with you as you move from chapter 1 to chapter 2? _____

_____

_____

_____

_____

_____

CHAPTER 2

The Field of Boaz

As we begin the second chapter of our story, we have to remember what has already transpired. The demise of Elimelech's family in the land of Moab has led a Jewish widow and a proselyte daughter-in-law to return to a land where a famine has recently lifted. The harvests would be particularly satisfying to the Israelites after they had suffered through such a tough time of need. Now, Naomi and Ruth are arriving back in Bethlehem of Judah as the first grain was gathered and the dormant winter season gave way to the new life of spring.

This was a time of great celebration on the heels of a season where everyone had to find a way to survive. A comparison can be found in the American survivors of the Great Depression. These people learned to live on very little and carried that ethic into a season of prosperity. Although they had much, they lived with the fear that it could be lost in circumstances beyond their control at any moment. It was a justified fear because they had just experienced those exact circumstances.

I remember sitting in the living room of my wife's grandfather's house. He was a depression-era kid who was born, had lived, and eventually died on the same dirt road in Mississippi. He lived in an incredibly humble home that had a total of six rooms. Straight lines and square

MY NOTES

corners had long since disappeared from the structure (if they had ever existed), and life was a very simple repetition of the same daily routine.

On the day we were visiting, Pa (that's what everyone in the family called him) received a survey in the mail that requested his opinion about some topic. The envelope that contained the survey had a cellophane window on its face with two pennies showing through the clear surface. Above it was the adage, "Give us your two cents' worth." I sat in Pa's little living room and watched as his arthritic fingers worked for half a minute or so to free the two pennies from their container. Once they had been dislodged, he slipped them into his pocket and discarded the envelope in the trash—where it should have been in the first place. My wife spoke up and said, "Did you get those pennies, Pa?" He answered with a statement that embodies the ethic of his generation: "Yeah, I did. Those pennies make dollars." With that commentary, he shook the front-right pocket of his overalls to reveal a wad of coins that probably totaled five dollars.

I thought about how many times I've purchased a coke from a convenience store and been offered some pennies as change. I remember many occasions where I've told the clerk to "keep it" because my generation's ethic says that the pittance of change is not worth the inconvenience it takes to carry it around. What a stark mental contrast.

So, Ruth and Naomi return to a post-depression (post-famine) culture with much less in their possession than those in Judah—who had little. Let's pick up our story and see how things unfold.

> **2:1** | "There was a relative of Naomi's husband, a man of great wealth, of the family of Elimelech. His name *was* Boaz."

We begin the second chapter with the introduction of our hero, Boaz! His name means "strength" and his introduction was accompanied by a description that says he was "a man of great wealth." However, this description is rendered in English several different ways, depending on the translator. For instance, some translators think that it is better rendered, "a great man of wealth." It only changes how we see the description slightly, but I'm pointing it out so that you can read the phrase with a little fuller understanding of what it could possibly mean. Let me continue to explain. Boaz was a great man. And he also had great wealth. Hence, he was great as a man, *and* he was great in the area of wealth. Other interpreters bring this description forward as "a great man of war" or "a great man of the law." The definitive meaning is not clear. But that's not necessarily uncommon when you're trying to get ideas to move from one language to another.

I read this variation of interpretation and find myself choosing, "D: all of the above." Boaz, who would become the redeemer for Ruth and Naomi, has often been compared to Christ, who redeemed believers through His death and resurrection on our behalf. As previously stated, he was a great man of war, law, and/or wealth. Or, if you want to say it this way, Boaz was the representation and embodiment of strength, wisdom, and provision.

Boaz was related to Naomi by marriage. It's interesting to me that both Naomi and Ruth are going to be related to Boaz by marriage before this story is over (spoiler alert). Since we the Church are now the Bride of Christ, it seems fitting that we have multiple characters that find their relationship to our hero through marriage.

Finally, I think it's interesting that this chapter opens with the introduction of Boaz. If we, being Western thinkers, were writing the story,

MY NOTES

we would probably introduce verse two and three before we introduce verse one because we put such great weight on circumstances. We would most likely talk about the circumstance in which our characters are introduced and then we would walk this new character into those circumstances. As a matter of fact, the story sort of unfolds that way in chapter one. We have our characters and events established early on, and then when it is time to introduce new characters, Orpah and Ruth, they are introduced based on the circumstances that surround our known characters. However, as this chapter opens, we find the most important person in the story, Boaz, getting the most prominent position. It's almost as if the writer is saying, "Before we go any further, I must introduce you to Boaz. He is the central figure of this story, and you need to know who he is before I begin to tell you the circumstances that bring his involvement into play." So now that we know who Boaz was, let's move on with the *happenings* of the story.

> **2:2-3 |** "So Ruth the Moabitess said to Naomi, 'Please let me go to the field, and glean heads of grain after *him* in whose sight I may find favor.' And she said to her, 'Go, my daughter.' Then she left, and went and gleaned in the field after the reapers. And she happened to come to the part of the field *belonging* to Boaz, who *was* of the family of Elimelech."

Ruth came to her mother-in-law and asked her permission to go and glean from the fields. Just that statement raises a couple of huge questions that can be answered with a basic understanding of the Hebrew law. For starters, why would a woman who is starving ask her mother-in-law (who is also starving) if she could go get food? Do you notice the conspicuous absence of other characters in this dialogue?

MY NOTES

Where are Ruth and Naomi living? The text doesn't tell us that. Are they squatting on some abandoned property? Are they living with some relatives? Evidently not. Are they taken in by some friends of the family from their life before Elimelech took them to Moab? We don't really know. However, we can make some assumptions: Wherever they are, it's not a permanent solution. Their needs are not being wholly provided for because Ruth was looking for food. As the story unfolds, we'll see Naomi get *very* excited at the prospect of Ruth meeting Boaz because it infuses hope into the situation.

The next revealing thing about this question from Ruth is the qualifier that Ruth puts on the end: "after him in whose sight I may find favor." Remember Naomi's argument earlier? She has no sons or grandsons to offer up as a potential "kinsman-redeemer" for Ruth. And now, her only daughter-in-law (that is, that's still around) is asking if she can "put herself back on the market" so to speak and find a husband. This would work out great for Ruth if it happened, but it would leave Naomi in a position of having no male heir to carry on the family name and no real sense of security for her old age. Ruth realizes the weight of her request. So, her love for Naomi compels her to get Naomi's blessing before she heads off to the fields to reap. In essence, Ruth is saying, "Hey, can I go to the fields to reap grain so that we'll have something to eat? And, in the meantime, I may be in the position of becoming attractive to whomever I meet there." Now, you have to think that as loyal as Ruth has been to Naomi, at this point she is probably depending on God to provide a way for both her and Naomi to find provision. Remember her pledge from chapter 1? She has committed to live and die with Naomi, and I don't think she had changed her mind at this point. The downside from

MY NOTES

Naomi's viewpoint was that this will most probably be the death of her hope for the Levirate Law to provide her with an heir.

Next, we need to understand what is happening here when Ruth asks to go "glean in the field." Ruth has obviously been captivated by the Hebraic system of living. She had the opportunity to abandon Naomi and return to her people, but she chose to go back to Bethlehem, Judah, and embrace the people and the God of Judaism. She is aware of the Levirate Law, and now makes it evident that she is also aware of the Hebrew (Levitical) Laws for provision. You see, in Leviticus 19:9-10, God sets up a system of welfare for the poor of the community. His system does not have the government handing out "money for nothing," but mandates that the owners of the fields where the grain is grown are to leave about thirty percent of what could be gleaned (extracted) in the fields. They are to leave the edges and the corners untouched, and they are not supposed to pick up anything they drop. The idea is that the owners will get first pass at the provisions, but then the people who do not own land could have a chance to recover what is left.

So, armed with the knowledge of this Law, Ruth sets out to find a field to glean in. Don't let the way the second chapter introduces itself to you in the first three verses fool you. Boaz is not yet in the story. He was *introduced* as a character when the chapter started, but that is only so we'll know who he is when his interaction with the others begins in the next verse. What I want us to see is that Scripture records that Ruth "happened" to come upon the part of the field that belonged to Boaz.

I cannot recall the number of conversations I've had with people about "coincidences," where the big question is whether God directs every step of our lives or if some things are just "coincidental." I am also unable to recall all the conversations I've had with people who

MY NOTES

complain about the fact that God doesn't direct them, speak to them, or get involved in their lives. Well, just look at verse three and all those arguments disappear. There is no indication that Ruth prayed fervently for the direction of God and then received special instructions for her life. She simply got up and did what had to be done and God showed up without her awareness. It's amazing how God will direct things if we'll just get moving. I'm not advocating that we give up praying for God to reveal His will in our lives. I'm only stating that when we expect God to speak in a certain way, or act in a certain way, we box Him in to our own expectations. We rarely hear His voice in that scenario because we're listening on the wrong channel. This reminds me of something I heard a preacher teach one time: He said that discovering the will of God in your life can be likened to driving a tractor. He asked, "How hard is it to steer a tractor that isn't moving? And how hard is it to steer one that is moving? Get moving and trust God to steer—or stop you if you're going too fast in the wrong direction."

Things don't just "happen." God knows our choices before we make them. But that doesn't make them less ours. God includes our choices in a design that includes His will, our will, and Satan's tactics. (If you really want to dive deeply into this concept, look up a Spanish Jesuit theologian named Luis de Molina, and read how he weaves the concepts of sovereignty with free will with the element of middle knowledge. It will help you solve the schism that many people face when they believe that the only two viable approaches to hermeneutics are found in Calvinism and Arminianism.)

Ephesians 2:10 teaches us that we are God's workmanship. The word used is "poiema," and we get our word "poem" from this Greek word. It is literally a "woven tapestry." The promise of Romans 8:28-29

MY NOTES

is that all of these things are worked together for the good of those who love God. He uses every circumstance, choice, and happening (whether we think of them as good or bad) to weave a perfect poem that He calls our life. Ruth is simply being navigated through the threads of life so that God can create a beautiful, poetic picture of His love for us. So with that understood, let's get further acquainted with our hero, Boaz.

> **2:4** | "Now behold, Boaz came from Bethlehem, and said to the reapers, "The LORD *be* with you!" And they answered him, "The LORD bless you!"

Whenever Scripture uses the word "behold," I always pause. To behold something is to see it as fully as possible—not just a glance. The only way to fully see a thing is to look—and I mean really look. So, this is like interrupting whatever Scripture is saying to yell, "LOOK!" and then completing the thought. "Behold" is always a biblical cue to pay special attention. In this passage, we see the writer saying to "pay attention," as Boaz appears on the horizon of our story.

So what do we see when we give this verse our attention? "Boaz came from Bethlehem." Boaz means "strength." Jesus (our Lord) is our strength and shield (Psalm 28:7). Boaz's greeting was, "The LORD be with you." I know that this is how the New King James translation states it, and I'm not trying to pretend that I'm even able to have a "translation" conversation with people who have dedicated their life to this business. But look at the verse closely. Anytime you see a word in the Bible that has been written in italics means that the English language does not have any equivalence to the Hebrew, Aramaic, or Greek text. The word "be" is not in the original text. The Hebrew language doesn't really allow for the "to be" (infinitive) verb. It's simply implied in the

MY NOTES

verb tense. The Hebrew language only requires that a sentence have a subject and a predicate. Consequently, the phrase would be literally re-phrased in English, "The LORD with you," or even more literally, "The LORD with." The words written in Ruth 2:4 therefore can be summed up as, "YHWH 'im.'" Isn't that (figuratively) one of the names referencing the coming Christ? Doesn't "Emmanuel" mean "God with us?" The literal wording of this phrase strikes me deeply. This book is laden with prophetic and typological (Please don't be thrown off by that word if you don't know it. It's just a way of saying that something in the text is a picture of something yet to come in the text.) inferences to the Truth that is yet to come. It's as if the author is transparently reminding us that God (YHWH) is sovereignly guiding every aspect of this story so that we can take confidence in the fact that He does the same for us.

The response of Boaz's workers was immediate. Their words are familiar because they remind us of the words spoken by Moses in Numbers 6:24. In that text, God had just spent an entire chapter describing the way a man should live if he was under the Nazarite vow. Then God turned back to Moses and said to tell Aaron and his sons that this was the way they were to bless the children of Israel. They would say, "The LORD bless you and keep you." Over time, it appears that this blessing became shortened and was a proper response to a greeting. It's not dissimilar to folks in the South saying, "God bless you" casually in their conversations. However, let's look just a bit closer at the wording.

The word for "bless," in this phrase, is "Barach" or "Baruch." Typically, this word is descriptive of people who are speaking of their position as they approach God. For instance, David said, "Bless the LORD, O my soul; And all that is within me, *bless* His holy name!" (Psalm 103:1).

MY NOTES

The word "barach" means "to kneel or bow." There is another word for bless in the Hebrew language. It is "Ashar," and it means "to be set upon the straight path." It is strikingly similar to the name of one of Jacob's (Israel's) son, Ahser, which means "happy." From a Western perspective it would make sense for the greeting to be, "The LORD set you upon a straight and happy path." However, when we look at what was instigated by God through Moses as the way to bless the children of Israel, it is this: "The LORD 'kneel down,' or 'stoop down,' to you." Doesn't that sound strikingly similar to the language we get when we transliterate the names of the first ten generations of man contained in Genesis 5 and 1 Chronicles 1:1-4? If we take the time to move each Hebrew name into its English equivalent, we see the gospel story hidden in the genealogical text. Chuck Missler *(Learn the Bible in 24 Hours)* does a wonderful job of transliterating the names of those first ten generations of man to show that even genealogies can hold prophetic reassurances of God's sovereignty and purpose for us. It's worth taking the time to discover. But for this discussion, we can simply focus on the names "Mahalalel" and "Jared." Transliterated, they can mean, "The Blessed God" and "He shall descend." So when we see the greeting offered in the Hebrew culture—or more specifically offered in this verse of Ruth—we see the hope of salvation embodied in a simple greeting. May God descend—stoop down—to touch your life.

Doesn't this exchange of greetings make for a beautiful picture when you put them together? Here's how it looks to me: Boaz, our type for Jesus, approaches his servants (God's Church) as they are tending to his fields, which are "white for harvest" (John 4:35). In essence, Boaz states, "Emmanuel, I am with you," and they respond, "May God the Father stoop down to touch your life." I like that picture. What I like even

MY NOTES

more is the picture of interaction drawn in the verses to come. Let's take a look.

> **2:5** | "Then Boaz said to his servant who was in charge of the reapers, 'Whose young woman *is* this?'"

The formalities of greeting are out of the way, and Boaz immediately gets down to business. This is another brilliant example of Scripture's ability to utilize the "economy of words" in a story, and then wait for us to discover all that is being said without actually being said.

First, Boaz spoke directly to his servant, and note that the dialogue is not a series of tasks or to-do's. He starts a friendly conversation and shows his humanity. He isn't interested in business first—he's interested in relationships. So often we get the idea that Christianity is first and foremost a list of dos and don'ts when, in truth, it's about relationships with Jesus. I'm not saying that we don't have tasks given to us and that work is not a part of the equation. I'm only saying that we work from a position of gratitude—and that gratitude is born out of relationships.

Next, Boaz shows his humanity again by asking about the young woman. She has caught his eye, and he makes no bones about it. He doesn't try to hide his interest in her by covering it with small talk, which could be construed as manipulative. You can almost see him "buddying up" to his most-trusted servant and saying, "Hey, who's the new girl—and has anybody spoken for her?" In the same way, Christ showed His humanity for us as He fell deeply in love with us. We are the "apple of His eye," and He paid a great price to win our love.

Next, Boaz attaches possession to Ruth's life by asking, "*Whose young woman is this?*" So often sin breeds a notion of independence in us that we simply cannot shake it. We are raised with the idea that "I

MY NOTES

am my own man or woman." But the truth is found more accurately in an old Bob Dylan song, "Gotta Serve Somebody," when he sang, "You're gonna have to serve somebody; Well, it might be the devil and it might be the Lord; But you're gonna have to serve somebody." Knowing this, we are able to make ourselves available to either master. One master seeks to steal, kill, and destroy, while the other seeks to offer life and life abundantly (John 10:10). And yet the lie of the master who seeks to kill is so enticing and so familiar that we often find ourselves drawn to its allure. Satan told Eve that she and Adam would not surely die by eating from the tree of the knowledge of good and evil. They would become like God (Genesis 3:4). He tells us the same thing: "You can be your own God. You can set your own course and design your own destiny." Our sinful heritage breeds in us the desire for that statement to be true. And we can spend our entire earthly existence under the influence of that attraction. We should give thanks for a Savior who redeems us out of that independent position and buys our freedom from death, despite our failings. We should live our lives amazed by Jesus, who desires a relationship of love far greater than He desires an arrangement of performance. He truly is a loving Master who calls us friend.

Isn't this the picture we see here as the master, Boaz, draws near to his servant to inquire about the young woman who has caught his eye?

> **2:6-7 |** "So the servant who was in charge of the reapers answered and said, 'It *is* the young Moabite woman who came back with Naomi from the country of Moab. And she said, "Please let me glean and gather after the reapers among the sheaves." So she came and has continued from morning until now, though she rested a little in the house.'"

MY NOTES

This "servant who was in charge" is way ahead of Boaz: He already knows her name and has had a conversation with her. He has obviously been watching her because Boaz asks her name, but the servant replies with her name, her home country, her request, and her activity for the day. He tells Boaz twice that she is from Moab. Evidently despising her country of origin was not enough to cause these men to turn away from her, and she obviously had some attractiveness about her that drew these men in. There was something very beautiful about Ruth that caused the first question of Boaz to be centered on her and caused the servant to have a comprehensive answer ready to deliver.

Beyond that, I can't help but notice that the servant says, "she rested a little in the house." There was nothing in that gleaning law that required a landowner to allow the poor to take up rest in their homes. You start to get the picture that this servant of the master saw the same beauty in the Gentile woman that Boaz saw, and he had already shown her kindness before Boaz even came on the scene. In the same way, when the Spirit of God (yes, I believe the "servant in charge of the reapers" had the same traits of the Holy Spirit and is a type for Him) begins to woo a non-believer into seeking life, do we not see in them the same beauty that Christ sees? Are we not supposed to use the provisions of the Master to comfort them and meet their needs until they ultimately meet the One who has provided for their rest and sustenance?

> **2:8-9 |** "Then Boaz said to Ruth, 'You will listen, my daughter, will you not? Do not go to glean in another field, nor go from here, but stay close by my young women. Let your eyes *be* on the field which they reap, and go after them. Have I not commanded the young men not to touch you? And when you

MY NOTES

> are thirsty, go to the vessels and drink from what the young men have drawn.'"

Commentators have much to say about these two verses. They tell us that the times were dangerous, especially for a widowed foreigner. Landowners were forced to allow them to glean in their fields, but they didn't necessarily like it. It was a common practice for a poor stranger to be met with insult and injury when they attempted to take advantage of this law.

So, what do we notice in this passage? We already know that even though these are the dark days of the Judges, Boaz was a godly man. His greeting to his servants and their return to him both center around the God who ruled their life. We know that they did not despise the Laws of God, because the servants didn't run Ruth off with insult or attack. We know that there had been much to do when Ruth and Naomi had shown up in town, and evidently Boaz's house had already heard about this "Moabitess" who had come home with Naomi (he addresses that in verse 11). This is what shaped Boaz's opening words to Ruth when he said, "You will listen, *my daughter*" (v. 8, emphasis added). He indicated from the opening greeting that he was already aware of who she was, and he told her that there was a tie of kinship between them. Remember, while Boaz knew who Ruth was, Ruth had just "happened" into a field not knowing that it belonged to a relative of Elimelech and Naomi.

We find Boaz going directly to Ruth and giving her "orders" to stay in his field. He didn't send word through a servant that it was okay if Ruth wanted to stay; he went to her directly and told her to stay in his fields to glean. And he even told her to connect herself to *his* young women. Just as an aside, I think it's funny that he told her to hang out with the

MY NOTES

young women instead of entrusting her to this leader of the servants that he had just been talking to. Boaz is showing a touch of jealousy for Ruth's attention, and he doesn't want there to be any confusion about his intentions. He entrusts her to the company of the young women who will teach her the ways of a young Hebrew woman.

Next, he told her to that she was to watch the fields that the young women work in and do what they do. If you'll remember, the Hebraic Law allowed for the poor to glean the corners, the edges, and the leftovers. But here we read Boaz instructing Ruth to glean in the fields *next* to his young women. That means that he is *including* her in the main harvest, instead of relegating her to the edges and corners. He also told her that when she was thirsty, she should drink from the water that the young men had drawn. Now, culturally speaking, drawing water from a well was women's work. I cannot find a commentator who discusses this peculiarity, so I'm not sure what to make of it. I can tell you that I have found multiple Scriptures that discuss women coming out to the wells in the evening and in the morning to draw water, but I cannot find a single Scripture about men drawing water from a well except right here. Yes, there is the verse in Luke 22 where Jesus instructs His disciples to follow the man who is carrying a pitcher of water—and the inference might be that the man had drawn that water from a well. But in the end, the text doesn't say that he drew the water. It only says he was carrying it. Anyway, I'll let you dig in on this one and find out what was going on. I have no real answers right now—it just caught my attention, so I know there is something here. Let me know what you come up with. I'd love to know your insight.

MY NOTES

> **2:10** | "So she fell on her face, bowed down to the ground, and said to him, 'Why have I found favor in your eyes, that you should take notice of me, since I *am* a foreigner?'"

Those who know the nuances of Hebrew language (not me) say that there is a hidden play on words here between the phrases "notice *of* me" and "a foreigner." They say that a rough English equivalent would be "respect a reject." If we catch this recognition of Ruth's view of herself, then we can begin to understand her response to Boaz's commentary. Let's really look at what's happening here.

A woman, who was in danger by just going out to gather food as an impoverished foreigner, "happens" upon the one field where a man not only allows her to pick through the leftovers but also gives her a crack at the first pass, numbers her among his own, and provides water and protection for her as if she was a member of his family. He even calls her "daughter." She, on the other hand, saw herself as a foreigner who was starving to death and wouldn't even be out there taking a chance if her life, and the life of her mother-in-law, didn't depend on it. To expect ridicule and maybe even punishment and then to be met with this sort of kindness was more than she knew how to deal with. She hits her face in bewilderment and asks the most obvious question: "Why have *I* found favor in your eyes?"

Fully grasping the importance of this verse can set us all free—if we allow it. Ruth saw herself as a foreigner, a reject, one who had no claim of any sort. Boaz saw her as a beautiful young treasure who was to be sought after and cared for. So often we have difficulty accepting Christ's gracious offers of mercy and acceptance because of how we see ourselves. We can't see value in ourselves, so we do not believe

MY NOTES

that Christ can see value in us. We define ourselves by our own opinion and we refuse to accept His opinion as a more accurate statement of eternal truth. When the day comes and we are able to say, "I may be a rejected foreigner on my own, but in Christ I am a treasure, a thing of beauty," we will find freedom. On that day, we'll acquire an inner-strength that can never be generated by pursuing accomplishments or treasures in the world system. It is an inner confidence that rests firmly in the knowledge that, "No matter what, I know that my Savior loves me." That is freedom!

> **2:11-12** | "And Boaz answered and said to her, 'It has been fully reported to me, all that you have done for your mother-in-law since the death of your husband, and *how* you have left your father and your mother and the land of your birth, and have come to a people whom you did not know before. The LORD repay your work, and a full reward be given you by the LORD God of Israel, under whose wings you have come for refuge.'"

This is an amazing response—I mean it. When you think about the way Boaz responds and compare it to the way that you or I would most likely respond in the same circumstances, it's amazing. "What is so amazing," you might ask?

First, Boaz began his response by countering Ruth's defeated and demeaning self-examination with truth intended to build up her self-confidence. He reminded her of the loyalty that she had shown to Naomi in the face of crisis. In the same way, we are repeatedly instructed to do all we can to edify and encourage one another. He didn't "flatter" her—which is hollow and self-serving. He edified and encouraged her

MY NOTES

with truth! It's paramount that we understand the difference and practice that difference in every relationship we have. However, it is equally imperative that we train ourselves to recognize the difference between "conviction" and "condemnation" that is so often expressed in the voice of the person we are trying to encourage. Conviction is "to be found guilty," but condemnation is "to be sentenced to punishment." We, as believers, are often convicted of our own sin, but we are not eternally punished. Christ took care of that for us. But we can easily fall into the trap of listening to a voice of condemnation and believing that it's true. This is the position that we see Ruth displaying in the previous passage. When we allow Satan to convince us that our guilt (according to the Law) is the determining factor in our relationships to God, we become ineffective and disconnected from the source of Grace that allows us to live life abundantly. Boaz corrects this judgmental, self-condemning thought process by interjecting thoughts of the true, noble, just, pure, lovely, virtuous, and praiseworthy (Philippians 4:8) decisions that Ruth has already made in her life. Satan condemns; the Word of God *commends*! Acts 20:32 says, "So now, brethren, I commend you to God and to the word of His grace, which is able to build you up and give you an inheritance among all those who are sanctified."

Secondly, Boaz took no credit for his kindness. Look at his response: He commended Ruth for her own selflessness and then turned all credit for blessings to God the Father. He says, may "*The* LORD repay your work" and may "a full reward be given you by *the* LORD God of Israel" (emphasis added). To top off the whole thing, he doesn't even take credit for giving protection and provision to Ruth! He finishes this statement by saying it was *God's wings* where Ruth sought refuge.

MY NOTES

Now, I don't know about you, but I would have most likely been tempted to answer this show of gratitude with a self-congratulatory pat on the back. I would have responded, "It's okay, Ruth. *I've* got you now. You have nothing to worry about while you're in *my* protection. God has richly blessed me, and *I am* able to provide for all your needs." But not Boaz! Look at his willingness to turn all attention to God. In the same way, Christ took no credit for Himself. He sought no glorification for Himself. Even when He cried out for God to glorify Him, He did it in a way that totally depended on God. Jesus sought the glory that comes from being with God. John 17:5 says, "And now, O Father, glorify Me with Yourself, with the glory which I had with You before the world was."

In addition, when Jesus speaks of the coming Holy Spirit, He said that the Spirit would glorify Him. You see, Jesus never took opportunity to glorify Himself. He waited for God to decide when the time for glory was right and simply walked in obedience.

> **2:13** | "Then she said, 'Let me find favor in your sight, my lord; for you have comforted me, and have spoken kindly to your maidservant, though I am not like one of your maidservants.'"

I can't help but wonder if Ruth wasn't covering her bases here a bit. She fell on her face before Boaz and praised him, but he refused to acknowledge that he had done anything. He simply commended her to God. She responded with something akin to, "Yeah, okay, but I would like to find favor in your eyes too." She reminded him of the kindness that he had shown, for which she was thankful for it. However, she was still practicing this "self-definition" thing—and it was working against her.

MY NOTES

She ended this retort with the comment, "I am not like one of your maidservants." Ruth was very aware of the kindness of Boaz. However, she was a little slow to accept the fact that the "maidservants" were just as congenial. She called herself a "maidservant," so she *was* beginning to warm up to the idea that this was the intended position for her to play in Boaz's life. But she saw herself as different from the "maidservants" who already have an association with Boaz. I think this is pretty similar to the way modern people see the Church. May we never be the ones who generate those kinds of thoughts in the "Ruths" of the world, who simply want the protection and provision of a kinsman-redeemer.

The sad thing to me about this verse is that there is no response from Boaz; we only get an announcement that the next thing that happened is at mealtime. Maybe the conspicuous absence of a response is God acknowledging the fact that the acceptance of outsiders may always be a problem. The problem with the family of God not accepting everyone becomes an unanswered fact in a sin-influenced world, where people are more interested in protecting themselves than providing for others. Nevertheless, we see the continued kindness of Boaz poured out in the next verses.

> **2:14** | "Now Boaz said to her at mealtime, 'Come here, and eat of the bread, and dip your piece of bread in the vinegar.' So she sat beside the reapers, and he passed parched *grain* to her; and she ate and was satisfied, and kept some back."

Every now and then a verse pops up in this book that is so blatantly metaphoric that you just have to giggle. This is one of those verses. None of us need a degree from seminary to understand that Ruth is a type for the Church and Boaz is a type for Jesus. So what did Boaz say

MY NOTES

to Ruth when they sat down to eat? "Here's some bread and wine for you to have." Okay, the translation is "vinegar," but a quick look at the original wording clears up what was being said. The word is "chomez," (Ho-metz) and it means "soured wine." Remember our discussion of Passover and the ridding of chamez (Ha-metz) or leaven/yeast? Both words center on this concept of souring. So, although the translation is vinegar, Boaz is offering Ruth *bread* and *wine*. Jesus is offering the Church *bread* and *wine*. That's why I giggle.

Ruth ate the daily bread that was given to her and there was "bread enough and to spare" (Luke 15:17), because she held back some bread at the end of the meal to take home to Naomi. That wording "enough and to spare" was used by the prodigal son, when he considered the generosity of his father.

Here's one more observation: With Jesus, there is always bread enough and to spare. I think about a pastor friend of mine who experienced the heartbreak of watching a church reject the poor of his city—primarily a Native American population. They began to attend his services and, little by little, the predominantly Caucasian members in the church stop attending until the remnant finally confronted him. Their announcement was heartbreaking but not uncommon in the modern American church. They told him that they were fine with the idea of sending money overseas to help indigenous peoples, but "this was their church." They weren't okay with giving it to impoverished Native Americans. Selfishness is always based in greed; greed is always based in fear. However, when we begin to understand that there is always enough and to spare, we lose all sense of fear because we are guaranteed to have "enough." We can eat our fill, spiritually speaking, and have more than enough left over for those who are in need. The

MY NOTES

trick is in following the lead of our Savior who regularly withdrew to be alone with His Father. There is the supply, there is the key, and there is the Father who gives generously to all who ask.

> **2:15-16 |** "And when she rose up to glean, Boaz commanded his young men, saying, 'Let her glean even among the sheaves, and do not reproach her. Also let *grain* from the bundles fall purposely for her; leave *it* that she may glean, and do not rebuke her.'"

We might think that Ruth got up from the table and thought that she had really pulled a good one. She had managed to put some food back for Naomi and was going to go home with the goods. However, Boaz, even knowing that Ruth had put some back, gave instructions to the men to let her have the best crack at the grain in the field. As a matter of fact, he even instructed them to drop some of what they collected "on purpose" so that she could pick it up easily and gather more food with less work.

So, what was the "purpose" that Boaz had for causing food to drop into Ruth's path? She had come out of a season of want. She and Naomi were in dire straits and Boaz wanted to do away with the suffering. I find it interesting that those who were already part of Boaz's family were instructed to do the work and then leave the fruit of their labor for the ones who had a greater need. There are a couple of parallels here. You could see how this is a picture of the Church being benefited by the lives of the Jews, as well as seeing the Church, once established, benefiting the newer believers. In either case, Jesus is sensitive to the individual needs of each of those in His care. Boaz knew that the servants and maidservants of his family had no stress over food, clothing, and/or

MY NOTES

shelter. These were the basic things in life that they took great confidence in their master to provide. However, the younger in the faith had no such confidence built up. It is in the reception of abundance that they began to build that confidence. So, Boaz goes out of his way to make certain that Ruth had more than enough.

All of this, of course, is designed to woo Ruth closer and closer to Boaz. He is absolutely crazy in love with this girl and is doing everything in his power to win her love in return. Remember, this is also Jesus courting His Bride—us.

> **2:17-18** | "So she gleaned in the field until evening, and beat out what she had gleaned, and it was about an ephah of barley. Then she took *it* up and went into the city, and her mother-in-law saw what she had gleaned. So she brought out and gave to her what she had kept back after she had been satisfied."

This is quick, but I have to say it: Ruth took a chance! She stepped out because she was desperate, but the payoff was tremendous. Don't you know that the food they ate that night tasted especially sweet. Take a chance on Christ. Do something desperate! He'll meet you in the dangerous field, and you will come home with far more than you hoped!

One more thought: I think it's imperative to notice that Ruth was taking provisions home to Naomi. She made a promise—a vow—and she's living up to it. It's always going to be tempting to move away from our commitments to generosity when abundance begins to come our way. But we need to steal a chapter from Ruth's story right here and decide right now that any blessing we receive from God will still, ultimately, belong to God. It is entrusted to us for *His* purposes and we

MY NOTES

need to be as happy when it passes to another as we are when it is passed to us. Don't let greed steal the joy we are freely receiving and freely giving. It's my experience that the attempt to hold on to what is entrusted to you is much like the Israelites in the desert who tried to gather extra manna. If you hold it tight, it only rots. If you use what you have and trust that God will refill what you need, you'll experience a constant flow of living blessing that will sustain you and those around you for all of eternity.

> **2:19** | "And her mother-in-law said to her, 'Where have you gleaned today? And where did you work? Blessed be the one who took notice of you.' So she told her mother-in-law with whom she had worked, and said, 'The man's name with whom I worked today *is* Boaz.'"

I like the fact that Naomi was already pronouncing blessing on Boaz without even knowing who it was. I think it's interesting that people are so taken with kindness and goodness in people when all kindness and goodness is the result of God's abiding love within them. Naomi was overwhelmed with the result of Ruth's good treatment and pronounced blessings on the man who owned the field before she even knew it is Boaz. After all, this was probably not the outcome that either of them expected when Ruth originally asked Naomi's permission to go "glean in a field." These were tough times, but this was an abundant response. Isn't that just like God?!

> **2:20** | "Then Naomi said to her daughter-in-law, 'Blessed *be* he of the LORD, who has not forsaken His kindness to the

MY NOTES

> living and the dead!' And Naomi said to her, 'This man *is* a relation of ours, one of our close relatives.'"

I laughed out loud when I read this for the first time. I pictured a "stereotype" (or Hollywood portrayal) of a large southern grandmother in an apron dropping a fork on the dinner table and exclaiming, "Praise God and shut my mouth—God ain't forgot me yet!"

It takes a minute for Naomi to regain her composure after her exclamation, and then she told Ruth the good news. You see, Ruth *was* the recipient of Boaz's kindness, but she had no idea that Boaz could do so much more than what she had already experienced. Naomi then spills the beans and announced the good news to Ruth, and they begin to share in the excitement as the next verse picks up.

Before we continue reading, I have to say that we are guilty of playing the Ruth role. We often relish in what Christ has already done for us, but we don't have a clue what He is capable and desirous of doing in the future. Let's read on.

> **2:21** | "Ruth the Moabitess said, 'He also said to me, "You shall stay close by my young men until they have finished all my harvest."'"

Ruth begins to understand the possibility that is unfolding here, and she chimes in with even more good news. She told Naomi that she had been invited to stay connected to this family as one of those who live in the protection of Boaz's young men. I do find it interesting that Ruth did not mention that she was to stay in the company of the young women but rather, the young men. I think this is another glimpse

into the humanness of Ruth, as she finds the parts of the story that she is most comfortable with and conveys those pieces. We often do the same. Our desires and opinions often cloud our view of life. We tend to see "from our perspective." May God grant us the grace to see from *His* perspective more often—as well as the grace to accept what we see. You might want to take a minute and let that prayer sink in. It's not an easy one to pray. And it's even harder to walk out.

> **2:22-23 |** "And Naomi said to Ruth her daughter-in-law, '*It is* good, my daughter, that you go out with his young women, and that people do not meet you in any other field.' So she stayed close by the young women of Boaz, to glean until the end of barley harvest and wheat harvest; and she dwelt with her mother-in-law."

Naomi realizes the truth of the situation very quickly. She knew Ruth was not actually going to hang out with the young men, because that would be wholly inappropriate. She responded by saying that it was good for Ruth to go out with the "young women," even though Ruth said that she would be in the company of the young men. These two facets speak of both protection and community. Ruth saw the blessing of Boaz through *her* filter of circumstance and Naomi saw it through hers.

Next, Naomi said that it was good that the people do not meet Ruth in any other field. Literally, this wording means "that they do not fall upon you." Remember that although these people had the Law of God, this was the time of the Judges, which ended with the declaration that "everyone did *what was* right in his own eyes" (Judges 17:6). People were just as selfish and mean then as they are now. Although the Law of God made provision for the poor, the keeping of the Law fell to the

MY NOTES

people—and they did a poor job of walking it out. That's what makes Boaz stand out all the more. He knew the Law and he kept the Law; he even went beyond the Law to show mercy and grace to Ruth.

One other quick note here: Naomi called Ruth "my daughter" because of the relationship formed in marriage back in Moab. Earlier in this chapter, Boaz addressed Ruth the same way. Do you see a parallel being foreshadowed? Boaz did not try to hide his courting of Ruth—even from the start. His intentions were perfectly clear from his first words to the servant in charge. He honored God and turned his attention to the thing that caught his eye. In this verbiage, we see Ruth as both Child and Bride, just as the Church is today.

Finally, chapter 2 concludes by telling us that Ruth obeyed Boaz's instructions. Her gratitude for his kindness led her to respond with obedience. She saw the benefit in doing what he had commanded and gladly went along with his wishes. She found such contentment and fulfillment in her obedience that this season lasted all the way through the barley harvest *and* the wheat harvest. That's fifty days. Remember our lesson from Leviticus 23: This is the season of the first fruits, and it runs from Passover to Pentecost.

Last note: Remember when Ruth promised, "Wherever you lodge, I will lodge" (Ruth 1:16)? She made good on her promise! She dwelt with her mother-in-law.

Review: Chapter 2

There is an old adage that says, "The New Testament is in the Old Testament, concealed. And the Old Testament is in the New Testament, revealed." Ruth chapter 2 is full of examples that prove that adage to be true. So many of the details in this chapter serve as examples (types) or pictures of what is to come. As we review the chapter with the questions below, keep notes on how each character and element of the story represents the unfolding and eternal truth of God's love for us expressed in the life of Jesus.

1. What character was introduced in the first verse of the chapter 2? _____

2. Why is it important that this character is introduced in the opening to this chapter? _____

_____

3. What question does Boaz ask the "servant who was in charge of the reapers" (v. 5)? And why is that important? _____

_____

4. When we look for "types" in this story, who does the "servant who was in charge of the reapers" (v. 5) represent? _____

_____

5. When we look for "types" in this story, who does Boaz represent?
   _____
   _____

6. What lesson do we learn from the servant's answer to Boaz regarding the role of the Holy Spirit in the life of the called?
   _____
   _____
   _____

7. Why was it a dangerous proposition for Ruth to suggest to Naomi that she go into the fields and glean grain? _____
   _____
   _____
   _____

8. In verses 8-9, Boaz offered protection and provision to Ruth. How did Ruth respond in verse 10? _____
   _____
   _____
   _____

9. In verses 11-12, Boaz answered Ruth's question. In your own words, what was Boaz's answer? _____
   _____
   _____
   _____

10. In verse 13, how did Ruth respond to Boaz's positive commentary? How did that correlate to our relationships with Jesus?

_____

_____

_____

11. In verse 14, Boaz invited Ruth to dinner. What was served at that dinner? What does that represent in our current relationship with Jesus? _____

_____

12. How did that meal settle the "back-and-forth" conversation between Ruth and Boaz found in verses 8-13? _____

_____

_____

13. Why was it significant that Naomi said, "He is one of our close relatives" in verse 20? _____

_____

_____

_____

14. What life lesson has Naomi learned from her excursion to Moab that prompted her to say to Ruth, "Do not let people meet you in any other field" in verse 22? _____

_____

_____

_____

15. How would you summarize the happenings, insights, and lessons you are taking with you as you move from chapter 2 to chapter 3? _____

_____

_____

_____

_____

_____

_____

_____

CHAPTER 3

The Threshing Floor

Our story takes a good leap forward in time here. We ended chapter 2 with a scene of Ruth and Naomi dreaming about the possibility of life taking a turn for the good. They are celebrating the goodness of God. I love the fact that Naomi is crediting God for that goodness. She returned to Bethlehem recognizing God as Lord and hadn't forgotten that fact when hope appeared on the horizon. Remember that Ruth ran into all this hope on her first day looking for food. The barley harvest was in full swing, so we know that it was only the beginning of the harvest season we outlined earlier.

Now, we move to a different season: the threshing floor, which means that the harvest season is winding down. You see, the grain (barley and wheat) would have been collected during the seven to ten weeks harvest season and prepared (threshed) at the close of the season.

Here's how it worked: Landowners would have servants go into the field and collect or "harvest" grain with sickles. They would cut and bind the sheaves of grain into bundles that would be left to dry a bit. Those bundles would be collected and stacked at the edges of the field, where they would be loaded onto wagons or carried by hand to the threshing floor. As the harvest season drew to a close, the servants would go to

MY NOTES

the threshing floor and begin separating the grain from the stalks and chaff, so that the grain could be collected for storage.

The fields were in the valleys where water would be plentiful. The threshing floors, however, were often times located on top of the hills or mountains that surrounded the valleys. Threshing floors were large flat areas of ground, typically made of clay, that were circular and could measure up to fifty feet in diameter. A line of rocks would create a border for the floor, and the surface of the floor would be pounded flat and smooth. There were several methods of threshing—from walking on the sheaves of grain, to beating the sheaves with sticks, to pulling oxen within a circular motion in order to tread on the grain. But in the end, the goal was always the same: separate the grain from the stalks.

Not every threshing floor took advantage of the benefit of being located on top of a hill. Just consider Gideon in Judges 6. The benefit of locating a threshing floor on top of the mountain was that the setting sun would create a breeze that blew up the side of the hill and across the top. The grain would be gently tossed into the air, and the servant would use a winnowing fork or winnowing shovel to move it around. The chaff or "husk" surrounding the grain was much lighter than the grain itself, so the breeze would catch it and blow it away from the grain. The grain would settle quickly and end up on the floor for easy collection. This was the process of threshing and winnowing the grain.

It is important to note that the symbolism of this process is found often throughout the Bible.

Both Matthew and Luke wrote about the harvest and threshing process in the third chapter of their respective Gospel accounts. They wrote: "His winnowing fan *is* in His hand, and He will thoroughly clean out His threshing floor, and gather His wheat into His barn; but He will

MY NOTES

burn the chaff with unquenchable fire" (Matthew 3:12; see also Luke 3:17). It is on the mountain—which is an example for "kingdoms" in Scripture—that the grain is separated out.

Jesus spoke to His disciples in Matthew 13 about the harvest and said that the tares (those that look like wheat but do not produce grain) will be gathered separately from the true wheat. They meet the same end as the chaff—fire (see verses 24-30).

In I Corinthians 3, Paul gave us a picture of Jesus testing the work of each man to see if it can endure the test of fire. That which is useless is destroyed, but that which is precious is preserved.

In these three instances, we find the Lord of the Harvest removing any trace of imperfection from the perfected saints and the work of Christ through them.

In this chapter of Ruth, we will see the saving work of Jesus coming to fruition as the precious (Ruth) is gathered into the fold of Christ (Boaz) on the hill (Calvary) where the sacred is separated from the "world" of stalks and chaff. I mean, come on—that's just a beautiful picture! And just to say it again plainly: Yes, we will be completely cleaned of any trace of sin when the harvest of heaven happens. Not only will sin be removed from our record, but it will also be removed from our lives. Not only will sin be removed, the temptation to sin will also be stripped away, so that only what is pure and precious remains! That day is coming! God, please, make it soon!

> **3:1** | "Then Naomi her mother-in-law said to her, 'My daughter, shall I not seek security for you, that it may be well with you?'"

MY NOTES

Our chapter opens with Naomi becoming a bit pushy. Remembering all the way back to chapter one, you'll recall Naomi wishing that Ruth and Orpah would find rest in the homes of their husbands. Well, it's been seven weeks and Ruth has had ample time to find rest in the home of a husband. Boaz made his intentions known from the start. And, evidently, Ruth had not acted on the circumstances. There were a lot of reasons that would explain her hesitance. For instance, remember the pledge she made to Naomi? She had already proven repeatedly that she was sincere in that pledge, so she was probably a little slow to act on Boaz's kindness because she didn't know exactly what it would mean for Naomi. Grief is a difficult thing that takes time to settle, and Ruth might have been exercising compassion by moving on with life slowly as a way of considering the emotional needs of her mother-in-law.

In any case, Naomi was expressing her desires and attempted to "take control" of the situation, as it were. She made this announcement that she was about to get involved in Ruth's well-being by in a sense saying, "Hey, since it's obvious that you aren't going to act on Boaz's kindness, I'm going to do it for you." Besides, Naomi knew how to play this Hebrew game much more effectively than Ruth. She knew the subtle nuances that allowed a young woman to announce her reciprocation of intent. She was schooled in the Hebrew ways, and she was about to take her pupil to a new understanding of how things were done in this culture. In the same way, there is much that we the Church can learn from our friends in the Jewish community. But often times, we're a bit too proud of what we "know is right," and a little too slow to consider that there might be a fuller understanding of something or a different perspective that is equally valuable to the one we already hold. In short: Keep a firm grasp on truth and an open mind to

MY NOTES

correction and learning! It will serve us all well if we live with that combination of humility and integrity.

> **3:2 |** "Now Boaz, whose young women you were with, *is he* not our relative? In fact, he is winnowing barley tonight at the threshing floor."

I'm a sucker for wanting to see the story unfold when Biblical characters are talking to one another. I realize that Scripture doesn't convey facial expressions and conversational nuance, but I still imagine myself there—watching the whole thing unfold. So, what do I see? I see a pregnant pause as Ruth considers Naomi's offer from verse one. There was a meeting of the eyes and a smile as the two silently agreed that it's time to move on with things. They also agree that Naomi was the one who knew how this dance played out. It's almost as if Naomi had spoken a non-debatable point and Ruth had no possible rebuttal. Once sufficient time to consider this truth sunk in, Naomi continued.

With Ruth's unspoken consent evident in the moment, Naomi began to lay out the plan. You could almost insert the words, "Here's what we're gonna do" into the beginning of verse two. She began with the fact that Boaz was a relative, just to remind Ruth of the privileges inherent in that fact. I am reminded that we are created in God's image (Genesis 1:27), and Jesus is the express image of God (Hebrews 1:3). Relation between us is a foregone conclusion. And, yet, if Ruth does not (or we do not) claim that relationship, she (or we) will never benefit from it. We are all in the same position. If we do not claim our relationship and take advantage of the covenant that is inherent in it, we do not profit from its existence.

MY NOTES

Next, Naomi began to lay out the strategy. She pointed out that the relationship was the key, but there must be participation. She began by telling Ruth how to find Boaz. She was basically saying, "Boaz is the key to all you've ever dreamed of, and I can tell you how to find him." God grant us the grace to point those in search of Christ to the place where He is!

> **3:3** | "Therefore wash yourself and anoint yourself, put on your *best* garment and go down to the threshing floor; *but* do not make yourself known to the man until he has finished eating and drinking."

Pictures are replete in this verse, so let's walk through it slowly. Naomi told Ruth to do three things in the opening half of this verse. She said that she should: 1. wash herself; 2. anoint herself; and 3. clothe herself.

- 1. Ephesians 5:26 tells us that husbands should sanctify and cleanse their wives by *washing* them in the water of the Word.
- 2. It is the Spirit of the Lord who *anointed* everyone from Abraham to Moses to David to Jesus. It is also the Spirit of God who draws men to Christ and brings life to the Word of God, teaching us all we ought to do and bringing to remembrance the things of Christ (John 14:26).
- 3. Romans 13 and Galatians 3 both remind us that we are to "put on" (*clothe* ourselves in) Christ.

In short, we see a picture of a woman approaching her Savior by being washed in the Word, anointed by the Spirit and robed in Christ. Faith comes by hearing the Word; man is drawn by the Spirit; salvation comes as we are robed in Christ.

MY NOTES

In the second half of the verse, Naomi instructed Ruth on how to present herself as a servant of Boaz. She began with an exhortation that Ruth should not be pushy or arrogant about the matter. Rather, she should allow the master to have his evening and wait for the opportunity to receive his instructions in his own time. There is a lot to see in this process, so let's read on and see how the whole thing unfolded.

> **3:4 |** "Then it shall be, when he lies down, that you shall notice the place where he lies; and you shall go in, uncover his feet, and lie down; and he will tell you what you should do."

Now how does Naomi know that Boaz is going to lie down? That's an easy one, but we'll need to have a truer picture of the threshing process for that picture to become clear. So, here we go.

There is a lot of grain to be threshed—a lot! There's no way to get it done in a single night. And, if you'll remember, the servants were going to be dependent, at least in part, on the rising breeze of evening to get the job done. Therefore, they were going to work from the beginning of the breeze until the dying of the breeze. Then they have a meal of thanksgiving for what was collected that night.

Because there is a lot of grain, and because the times are evil, it becomes a prime opportunity for theft. To try and prevent robbers from taking away weeks of hard work, the men who were going to go to sleep encircled the grain at the edges of the threshing floor. They'll put their heads closest to the grain with their feet sticking out. From a bird's eye view, it would look sort of like spokes sticking out from a hub. This culture would have men sleeping on mats of some sort. Probably a skin of some type. They would be covered by skins as well to protect them from the cool of the night.

MY NOTES

Naomi told Ruth to wait until all the men went to sleep and then "uncover" the feet of Boaz and lie down there. This is a pretty unusual request. And, if you don't understand the culture, you may try to read something promiscuous into the scenario. There is a lot of commentary to be found on this verse, and I'll leave it to you to read the myriad opinions. But we're going to take a more virtuous view of the circumstances.

First of all, the men would have been fully clothed and fully armed in order to thwart any attempt at theft. Secondly, it was the law and custom of the time for a servant, whether male or female, to lie at the feet of the master and share in his bed covering.

When Boaz lied down for the night, he would have covered up fully to fight off the cool evening temperatures. Naomi told Ruth to uncover his feet and lay under the cover. This announced to Boaz that Ruth is presenting herself as his personal servant for as long as she lived. Remember when Boaz told her to stay close to his maid-servants? She assumed the position that they played in Boaz's life. Naomi also told Ruth that Boaz would know exactly how to react to this offer and would tell Ruth what to do next.

There it is folks: the process of being washed, anointed, and clothed in Christ, and then presenting ourselves for service in His kingdom. What a beautiful picture! However, the picture is far from over.

> **3:5-6 |** "And she said to her, 'All that you say to me I will do.' So she went down to the threshing floor and did according to all that her mother-in-law instructed her."

I spoke with a pastor friend of mine one time and asked him for some advice. He gave it to me, and I considered it. In truth, I didn't really do what he suggested because I got a bit lazy. Later I asked for advice

MY NOTES

again. He replied, "The last time you asked me what I thought you ought to do, you ignored what I told you. Why would I want to keep giving advice that will have no effect?"

Look at Ruth's response to Naomi's instruction: "All that you say to me I will do." *God, give us the heart to take instruction from godly counsel and follow it with true humility and submission.*

One more note: Jesus warned about a son who told his father that he would go into the field to work but then changed his mind and did what he wanted to do (Matthew 21:28-32). That's never a good combination. Jesus continued to speak about another son who initially refused to do the work his father sent him to do but then changed his mind and did what was requested. Jesus finished the parable by asking rhetorically, "Which of the two did the will of *his* father?" (v. 31). Here we have a young woman who not only pledges to do what was requested, but she followed through with that pledge with absolute obedience. She could have said, "Wait a minute. Explain to me why you're asking these things. Am I putting myself in danger here? How is Boaz going to respond? Help me understand and then I'll tell you whether I'll do it." How often do we want an explanation before obedience? *God, give us the grace to obey without hesitation, reservation, or explanation!*

> **3:7 |** "And after Boaz had eaten and drunk, and his heart was cheerful, he went to lie down at the end of the heap of grain; and she came softly, uncovered his feet, and lay down."

Just an aside here, Ruth waits until Boaz has had his celebratory dinner before she did what she was supposed to do. Remember that the men on the threshing floor would have done their work and then had a dinner of thanksgiving before God. I like the fact that Scripture

MY NOTES

records that Boaz's heart was cheerful. Psalm 104 tells us of bread that strengthens the heart, oil that makes the face shine, and wine that gladdens the heart. You see, these three things indicate the bounty of God. They received bread from a harvest of grain, oil from the olives, and wine from the grapes. Boaz was remembering the famine that had just passed and fell asleep with the knowledge that God had returned to their land with favor. In the same way, I can remember the agony that Christ suffered as He experienced the night before His execution. He knew that a season of famine was beginning the next day, and that He would be cut off from His Father—and *nothing* was more precious. The loving relationship that He had known from eternity would be barren to Him. And, yet, Jesus did not turn from the Lordship of God the Father. Neither did Boaz leave the land of Bethlehem during his famine time. However, there is coming a harvest! There is coming a celebratory feast in that harvest. It is the wedding feast of the Lamb where the fruit of Christ's labor will be gathered in. The grain shall be gathered, and the chaff and tares removed. That will truly be a time of celebration, followed by a time of rest!

In this verse we read something that may be construed as inappropriate: Ruth uncovered the feet of Boaz and laid there. However, if you have not read the notes of verse 4, I invite you to do so now. Although this act may seem like a forward and inappropriate action on her part, this was well accepted in the customs of the day.

One of the most beautiful things to me about this verse is that Ruth did not follow through with covering herself. She uncovered Boaz's feet and then simply laid down. She left the covering to him! She depended on *his* goodness to win out in *his* timing.

MY NOTES

Also, there is a descriptive phrase that gives us a good image of how this process began: Ruth waited until the supper was finished and all the men went to sleep. And then, "she came softly." Now, these guys were circled around the grain, fully dressed and fully armed, ready to defend against anyone who would try to steal their harvest. There are several lessons right there. Ruth, very quietly, approached Boaz's feet. There are people who believe that this is a very dangerous and daring move on her part. Women did not typically participate in the threshing. For a single woman to be in the midst of that many men in that type of environment opens up a ton of opportunity for impropriety and scandal. And, yet, Ruth's desire for Boaz was so strong that she took the risk. There are those who assume that Ruth did this thing late at night so that Boaz would be free to reject her without the whole town knowing her intent. Scripture doesn't provide details, and that is one of the things I love about it. The Spirit of God tells us what we need to know and then leaves us to dwell on the details of the story. In any scenario, it is clear that Ruth is being slightly daring and completely submissive. We'll see more of how this all plays out in the next couple of verses, so let's read on.

> **3:8-9 |** "Now it happened at midnight that the man was startled, and turned himself; and there, a woman was lying at his feet. And he said, 'Who *are* you?' So she answered, 'I *am* Ruth, your maidservant. Take your maidservant under your wing, for you are a close relative.'"

Well, here we go. Boaz was protecting the grain and he woke up because the blanket was no longer over his feet. He reached down to fix the problem and there was someone at his feet. The alarm sounds in

his half-awake brain and he was ready to fight. Then, he discovered that it was a woman at his feet and that made no sense at all. I mean, put yourself in his position. You're half-awake and half-asleep and nothing in your circumstance is making sense. So, he asked the obvious question, "Who *are* you?"

Ruth told Boaz that it was her (but finishes with a request that we'll talk about in a minute), which indicates that she had fully accepted her roles as "maidservant." Back in chapter 2, she accepts the fact that she was being made into a maidservant. But she finished her assessment by saying that she was not like the other maidservants. Here, she offered herself at the feet of Boaz as a maidservant. She had grander hopes for the night's outcome. She said, "Take your maidservant under your wing, for you are a close relative." In this moment, she was presenting herself as a candidate to become Boaz's wife. We know this by looking at additional Scripture that addresses her unusual actions, the meaning of the phrase "take your maidservant under your wing."

Ezekiel 16:8 is a relevant passage. It says, "'When I passed by you again and looked upon you, indeed your time *was* the time of love; so I spread My wing over you and covered your nakedness. Yes, I swore an oath to you and entered into a covenant with you, and you became Mine,' says the Lord God." The phrase "spread My wing" in this context refers to the corner of a blanket. Not only was it the right of a servant to cover himself with his masters covering (as we've discussed), but it was also a statement of intent for a man to offer the "corner" or "wing" of his covering to a young woman to express his intentions in marriage. It's sort of like a girl saying "yes" at the presentation of a diamond ring.

Just in case there is any doubt about what Ruth was asking or what Boaz was pledging, look at the last phrase. Ruth said, "For you are a

MY NOTES

close relative," reminding him of his legal right to claim her as a bride. His birth gave him the right to reclaim her under the Levirate Law that we discussed in chapter 1. In the same way, Christ's birth, life, death, and resurrection gives Him the right to redeem us as His Bride.

Finally, notice that Ruth followed Naomi's instructions and did this act in the dark, after everyone was asleep. She could have drug Boaz into the court that met at the city gate and demanded his redemption as the GO'EL, but she did not. She knew that the difference between them was evident, and she handled her business with gratitude. She was shown amazing kindness by this man, and she repaid that by allowing him to be the sole determiner of their future without coercion or pressure. Ruth presented herself in humility and quietness, and she was fully prepared to receive whatever answer came her way.

You need to know that there were options available to Boaz. So let's keep reading and discover what those options were, and what Boaz chose to do.

> **3:10** | "Then he said, 'Blessed *are* you of the LORD, my daughter! For you have shown more kindness at the end than at the beginning, in that you did not go after young men, whether poor or rich.'"

This word "kindness" is a tough one. There is a lot of nuances here that the commentators have much to say about. They write that it is very akin to the concept of "piety." You see, Ruth had already made her intentions as a prospective proselyte known by moving back to Bethlehem with Naomi. Her pledge to God was evident. She could have used that card to pursue a man more her age. However, she chose to respond to the kindness of Boaz, even though there are more "attractive" options.

MY NOTES

In Scripture we learn that there was nothing spectacular about the appearance of Christ that should draw anyone to Him—He was "common." Here we see a kinsman-redeemer (Boaz) who is evidently not the prize catch of his day, and yet his true beauty was undeniable by those who experience his love and protection.

When he said that Ruth had shown more kindness at the end than at the beginning, you have to remember all the way back to the pledge that Ruth made to Naomi. Boaz had already noticed her kindness to Naomi. And now he was saying that her choice of him was selfless and true. We have to admit that Boaz had much to offer (much more than any other prospect), yet he told Ruth that she could have gone after a young man who had physical (or temporary) beauty—but she did not. Her quest for a husband was completed in this act of asking Boaz if he would have her. It was the choice that would benefit *everyone* involved, and it's obvious that Ruth had considered more than her own selfish desires in this decision.

In the same manner, Scripture is redundant about the fact that people who come to Christ must consider everything fully. Salvation is not designed to bring people everything that they have ever wanted in this life. It is designed to be the most rewarding act of selfless obedience in which everyone could possibly participate. The reward of the Kingdom is not equal to the rewards of earthly systems. And compensation for loyalty does not come in the manner that the world seeks to be compensated. Our treasure is not of this world, and we are not to seek the temporal things that bring no true life. Like Ruth, we are to count the cost of our decision before making it.

A final note: We have grown comfortable with the fact that our request to Christ for salvation is a foregone conclusion. We get so

MY NOTES

comfortable with the fact that Jesus is going to accept us that we forget what a gift that acceptance actually is. In our story, Boaz could have said no. We have the ability to read Scripture and know that God has promised that He will accept all who call upon His name. However, we need to remain mindful that this acceptance is still an *amazing* gift of grace.

But, back to our story. Right now, Boaz had at least three choices. First, he could tell Ruth that what she was doing was inappropriate and send her away. Second, he could tell her to stay at his feet and he would provide for her and protect her as he did all of his maidservants. Or, third, he could do what she was requesting and begin the process of pursuing her as his wife under the Levirate Marriage Law. Which one would he choose? The answer is in the next verse.

> **3:11 |** "And now, my daughter, do not fear. I will do for you all that you request, for all the people of my town know that you *are* a virtuous woman."

Here is the response that we have come to depend on so desperately: Boaz said, "I will do for you *all* that you request" (emphasis added). Because Boaz is a type for Jesus, he responds the same way that Jesus promises He always will. In John's Gospel, chapters 14 through 16 show Jesus opening the line of communication with our heavenly Father. He says that we can ask the Father "in His name" and the Father will do all we ask (John 14:13-14). To further see the power of this name, we simply need to consider the fact that Jesus uses the phrase "in my name" seventeen times in the Gospels. There is power in the name of Jesus. However, we need to see with accuracy what is being said by Christ! A name was an indication of *character*. Christ is telling us that if we make

MY NOTES

a request of the Father, it needs to be made in the *character* of His life. Do not make a request of the Father that Jesus Himself would not make. Nevertheless, if we ask *anything* in the character (name) of Christ, the Father will grant what we ask. That's not a modern day "name-it-and-claim-it" theology of wealth and comfort. That's a promise that as we become more and more unified with the heart and mind of Christ, we can—and should—begin to pray the prayers that Jesus desires to pray in our circumstances.

> **3:12-13** | "Now it is true that I *am* a close relative; however, there is a relative closer than I. Stay this night, and in the morning it shall be *that* if he will perform the duty of a close relative for you—good; let him do it. But if he does not want to perform the duty for you, then I will perform the duty for you, *as* the Lord lives! Lie down until morning."

There is much to say about these verses, but I am going to withhold some of the conversation until we actually meet this "closer" relative. I'll only introduce the purpose of this relative here. He is never named in our story. Just as Boaz is an example or type for Christ, this closer relative is an example or type for the Law. We'll see how this plays out in the fourth chapter of our story. But, for now, just look at the submission that Boaz shows to the legal duties of this relationship. He is not usurping the closer relative. But he *is* going to win out in the end. Remember that Jesus said that He did not come to destroy the Law and the prophets; He came to fulfill them (Matthew 5:17).

Next, Boaz told Ruth that *if* this closer relative would perform the redeeming duties, he would allow him to do it. However, we all know that the Law is incapable of redeeming anything. The Law only exposes the will

MY NOTES

of God and the fallen nature of man (Romans 7:7). The Law is a tutor that teaches us about our sin and exposes our need for a savior—a redeemer.

Finally, look closely at the language in the last line. Boaz said, "*as* the LORD lives." However, notice that the "as" is in italics. It's not in the original language, but linguistically it is inferred. So what did he literally say here? He said, "I will perform the duty for you, the LORD lives." He was saying that his promise to Ruth was as sure as the very existence and nature of God. And then Boaz ended his response with a command to rest. Can't you hear Jesus answering the same way? Jesus is reminding us that He has given us His guarantee that He will redeem us—so rest!

> **3:14** | "So she lay at his feet until morning, and she arose before one could recognize another. Then he said, 'Do not let it be known that the woman came to the threshing floor.'"

Boaz's strategy is evident. He was going to give this closer relative (the Law) every chance to claim what was rightfully his to claim. However, Boaz—knowing the character of the closer relative—knew that the closer relative would pass on the opportunity and that would be his chance to rightfully and legally claim Ruth as his bride. But he also recognized that if word got out that Ruth came to the threshing floor at night, it could be construed as inappropriate. So he commands all the men at the threshing floor to keep their mouths shut so that he could protect Ruth's reputation while he went about the work of fulfilling his promise to her. I wish we could ingest the wisdom of this verse in our daily lives. How much grief could we put to rest—and how much peace could we propagate—if we would simply keep quiet regarding things that can unnecessarily tarnish a reputation? Proverbs 12:23 tells us that

MY NOTES

a wise man does not tell all that he knows. Let's be wise as we exercise kindness in our silence.

Okay, time to move on. Boaz had more instructions before he moved on with the duties of the day.

> **3:15** | "Also, he said, 'Bring the shawl that *is* on you and hold it.' And when she held it, he measured six *ephahs* of barley, and laid *it* on her. Then she went into the city."

So, what is the point here of the giving of grain? Boaz didn't just want to send Ruth away with a promise. After all he had done, that should be sufficient. However, Boaz was not interested in sufficiency—he was interested in abundance. He gave a deposit of his pledge to Ruth, and then he sent her away until this business of redemption was complete. The gift was a sign to Naomi and anyone watching the process that his intentions were true. In the same way, Christ's business of redemption will be complete when He comes back to claim His Bride. But until then, we are given the depository gift of the Holy Spirit.

> **3:16-17** | "When she came to her mother-in-law, she said, '*Is* that you, my daughter?' Then she told her all that the man had done for her. And she said, 'These six *ephahs* of barley he gave me; for he said to me, "Do not go empty-handed to your mother-in-law."'"

This verse emphasizes that this event took place early in the day. It was so early that Naomi wasn't even awake yet. She had to ask Ruth, "*Is* that you?" as Ruth came in the door. Immediately Ruth began to

MY NOTES

recount all that Boaz had done for her. She ended her account with the truth that Boaz had sent the gift to benefit both Ruth and Naomi.

We, as the Church, can sometimes think that this blessing we are afforded in Christ is strictly for us. But God's promises ran first to the Jew and then to the Gentile. Therefore, the gift of salvation is for all, and the deposit of salvation should benefit both the Jew and the Gentile.

> **3:18** | "Then she said, 'Sit still, my daughter, until you know how the matter will turn out; for the man will not rest until he has concluded the matter this day.'"

You know that Ruth had to be tempted to head off to the city gate and find a quiet place to watch this all go down. So often, we can be trapped into laying around in worried anxiety because we cannot see what is progressing—or how. Naomi was very explicit in her instructions to Ruth: *"Sit still."* She told Ruth that she was to wait quietly until the end of things was exposed. Then she ended the conversation with an assurance. She said, "The man will not rest until he has concluded the matter." What a promise for us to end chapter 3! Christ did not rest until the matter of our sin had been redeemed; Christ will not fully rest until the matter of our homecoming is completed.

MY NOTES

Chapter 3 Review

Chapter 3 is the most personal of the chapters in the Book of Ruth. It happens in the quiet of the night, and it unfolds as a personal and vulnerable interaction between Ruth and Boaz. As you work through the questions below, think of how you would use the insight God is providing to remember the intimate and personal way that God loves you. And then share that insight with other people who are looking for avenues to deepen their understanding of God, and their relationship with God.

1. The third chapter of Ruth opens with wisdom and guidance coming from which character? _____

   _____

2. What lesson do we learn about the study of Scripture from thinking about question 1? _____

   _____

   _____

3. In Ruth 3:3, Naomi instructed Ruth to do three things in preparation for the events that would follow that evening. What were those three things? _____

   _____

   _____

RUTH 3 REVIEW 153

4. Explain what the three things discussed in answer 3 represent to the believer—and to you personally. _____
   _____
   _____

5. Once Ruth was prepared according to the instructions given in verse 3, what did Naomi tell her to do next? _____
   _____
   _____

6. What was Boaz doing on the day that chapter 3 took place? ___
   _____

7. Explain the process of threshing grain so that you can help others understand the environment that Ruth was walking into as she approached Boaz. _____
   _____
   _____

8. Describe the scene that Ruth would have encountered when she arrived at the threshing floor. _____
   _____
   _____

9. Why would the men of Boaz's tribe be arrayed in the fashion that is described in verse 8? _____
   _____
   _____

10. What action did Ruth take when she arrived at the threshing floor? _____
_____

11. Boaz woke up at midnight and saw Ruth. What request did Ruth make of Boaz when he awoke? _____
_____
_____

12. Describe the three (or more) options available to Boaz once Ruth made her request. _____
_____
_____
_____

13. Explain the similarity between Ruth 2:12 and Ruth 3:9 and discuss the lessons we learn by comparing those two verses.
_____
_____
_____
_____

14. Boaz answered Ruth's request by saying that there was another who was a closer relative. Who was the closer relative (who is that "closer relative" a type for)? _____
_____
_____

RUTH 3 REVIEW

15. Boaz sent Ruth home early in the morning, but she was not empty handed. What did Boaz give her? What lessons do we learn from that gesture? _____

_____

_____

16. What instructions did Boaz give to the young men who were with him at the threshing floor when they woke up the following morning? Why do you suppose he gave that instruction? _____

_____

_____

17. When Ruth arrived home and told Naomi about the events of the previous night, what instructions did Naomi give? What assurances did she give to Ruth? _____

_____

_____

18. How would you summarize the happenings, insights, and lessons you are taking with you as you move from chapter 3 to chapter 4? _____

_____

_____

_____

_____

CHAPTER 4

The City Gate

As we begin our final chapter of this story, we need to understand the significance of the "gate." Chapter 1 takes place in Moab. Chapter 2 takes place in the harvest fields. Chapter 3 takes place at the threshing floor. Chapter 4 takes place at the city gate. This was the equivalent of the town council or city hall. Matters of importance were brought to the fathers of the community and settled here in a public forum. These were legal matters, and the decisions made here were final. We'll discuss the details of the proceedings as they unfold, but the important thing to remember is that Boaz called the closer relative into a court of law and settled this matter about Ruth once and for all.

"Now Boaz went up to the gate and sat down there; and behold, the close relative of whom Boaz had spoken came by. So Boaz said, 'Come aside, friend, sit down here.' So he came aside and sat down" (Ruth 4:1).

Boaz opens this dialogue by referring to the closer relative as a friend. I can't stress how important this is. So often, we think of the law as our enemy, but that simply is not the truth. The law is not sinful. Paul covers that comprehensively in his Romans discourse. Satan is the enemy. The law only exposes our inability to perform under the requirements of the commandments. But beyond that, the law is a reflection of who God is. Since Boaz was completely lawful in his dealings with

MY NOTES

Ruth and Naomi to this point, it was easy for him to refer to this relative as "friend."

> **4:2** | "And he took ten men of the elders of the city, and said, 'Sit down here.' So they sat down."

Boaz was completely disclosing to the onlookers. He placed judges in seats around him so that they would weigh the matter out and find the truth in these proceedings. In the same way, Jesus never hides anything for selfish advantage. His actions and motives are clear for all to see and to judge. All that Jesus does is within the Law and in accordance with the Spirit of the Law.

> **4:3** | "Then he said to the close relative, 'Naomi, who has come back from the country of Moab, sold the piece of land which *belonged* to our brother Elimelech.'"

The short paraphrase of this one is, "Naomi has sold her inheritance." Do you remember the story of the prodigal? He sold his inheritance as well. Scripture has several stories about inheritance and birthright being sold and *none* of them end well without the intervention of a redeemer!

It's also important to note that Naomi had "come back" from Moab. If she had stayed outside the family of God, the inheritance sold would have remained the possession of the purchaser. However, her repentance brings opportunity for reclamation and redemption.

> **4:4** | "And I thought to inform you, saying, 'Buy *it* back in the presence of the inhabitants and the elders of my people.

MY NOTES

> If you will redeem *it*, redeem *it*; but if you will not redeem *it, then* tell me, that I may know; for *there is* no one but you to redeem *it*, and I *am* next after you.' "And he said, 'I will redeem *it*.'"

Check this out carefully! Boaz offered the closer relative the first crack at buying back the land that Elimelech had lost. Remember that the Levirate Law protected two things: the family's seat at the city gate (which is a position of relationship) and the land that had been granted by God when the Israelites came into the promised land. That means that this Levirate Law dealt with *possessions* and *people*. Boaz began his conversation with the closer relative by discussing the *possessions* that were at stake.

Boaz points out that the closer relative had the first crack at redeeming the land if he was able and desirous. The relative speaks up quickly because he saw the value in the possession and says, in a sense, "*Yes*, I'll take it!"

> **4:5 |** "Then Boaz said, 'On the day you buy the field from the hand of Naomi, you must also buy *it* from Ruth the Moabitess, the wife of the dead, to perpetuate the name of the dead through his inheritance.'"

Now Boaz exposes the weakness in the Law—the closer relative. In a sense, Boaz was saying, "Okay, since you're going to buy the land, you need to know that there are strings attached. More accurately, there are *people* attached." This land was connected the family of Elimelech, which meant his sons also had inheritance. Since Naomi and Ruth

MY NOTES

were the survivors of that family, Ruth was attached to this deal. Boaz announced the obvious fact that Naomi was involved in the sale, but then also introduces the "string," if you will. Boaz reminded the closer relative with a, "Hey, don't forget that Ruth, *the Moabitess*, is attached to this deal. And that means when you buy the field, you get Naomi and *her*. If you buy this possession, you get all the people that come with it."

The closer relative would have no problem with purchasing the land and taking back Naomi. After all, she was a Jew, and that was honorable. However, taking charge of a reject, a foreigner, a "toilet-bowler" was abhorrent. If this relative bought back the possession, he got all the associated reputation that came with it.

This isn't dissimilar from the opening text of Luke 15, where the Pharisees mumbled against Jesus because He associated with sinners. In this society, if you wanted to ruin your life, all you had to do is associate with those below you in the social pecking order. This society ran on the paradigm of shame and honor. To accept an inheritance or to redeem an inheritance that included shameful Moabites was disgusting and would taint your entire life.

Let's look at how the Law—which must remain pristine—responds to this concept of accepting that which is tainted.

> **4:6** | "And the close relative said, 'I cannot redeem *it* for myself, lest I ruin my own inheritance. You redeem my right of redemption for yourself, for I cannot redeem *it*.'"

There is some amazingly important language right here, so don't miss it. The closer relative said two astounding things:

MY NOTES

- Accepting this opportunity for redemption would ruin his existing inheritance; all that he had become degraded or worthless if the redemption was tainted by anything impure.
- With an emphatic statement, the closer relative exclaimed, "I *cannot* redeem *it!*"

The Law is capable of conveying the nature and will of God. The Law is capable of exposing the fallen nature of man. However, the Law *can't* buy back the lost. The Law *can't* restore. The Law *can't* redeem. If the Law accepts anything that is not pristine and perfect, it becomes corrupt and can no longer be the Law of God. If the closer relative accepted a sinful Gentile, he would have become corrupted, and his entire life and reputation would be corrupted.

Scripture does not tell us the genealogy of Elimelech. I can only imagine that it had one significant difference from Boaz's genealogy. Do you remember who Boaz's parents were, because it's really going to matter as the story progresses? Boaz was the son of Salmon and Rahab, the gentile prostitute who gave shelter to the Hebrew spies in Jericho. So Boaz already had Gentile descent in his genealogy. I can only imagine that Elimelech's "closer relative" had a "pure" Jewish heritage. To willingly include a Gentile into his family line would taint his perfected roots, and that could not happen.

Here's what we learn in these few verses: The Law (the closer relative) is always interested in proper procedure. However, the Law is incapable of being interested in procuring people. Procedure over people, that is the core of religion and legalism. The Law is a legalistic, religious system that is designed to teach us just how desperate we need a Redeemer ... a Savior ... a GO'EL. Here we have a picture of the Law being incapable of doing what Boaz had already pledged to do.

MY NOTES

> **4:7-8 |** "Now this *was the custom* in former times in Israel concerning redeeming and exchanging, to confirm anything: one man took off his sandal and gave *it* to the other, and this *was* a confirmation in Israel. Therefore the close relative said to Boaz, 'Buy *it* for yourself.' So he took off his sandal."

Man, is this ever a watered-down version of the actual Law—and a perfect example of how man tries to make "customs" that are easier to swallow than the Law! The real Law is found in Deuteronomy 25:9, and it is far more humiliating and harsher than the "custom" outlined in verse 7. Deuteronomy 25:9 says that the widow of a deceased Jewish man may *require* the GO'EL to redeem her. And, if he refuses, she can take his sandal and then gets to spit in his face. Shoes were a sign of nobility. Only noblemen—blessed men—wore shoes. So to take a man's sandal is to remove his dignity and standing with God. And spitting in his face? Well, we don't really have to comment on that one, do we?

In this version, you see the closer relative sort of sheepishly giving up and handing over the shoe. It's kind of like yelling *Uncle* before the fight even begins. He was whipped from the start because wherever the Law exposes sin and causes it to abound, *grace* abounds more!

> **4:9-10 |** "And Boaz said to the elders and all the people, 'You *are* witnesses this day that I have bought all that was Elimelech's, and all that *was* Chilion's and Mahlon's, from the hand of Naomi. Moreover, Ruth the Moabitess, the widow of Mahlon, I have acquired as my wife, to perpetuate the name of the dead through his inheritance, that the name of the

> dead may not be cut off from among his brethren and from his position at the gate. You *are* witnesses this day.'"

Do you see all that is here? If you're not pumping your fist into the air with excitement right now, then you might not truly see what has just happened. The closer relative (the Law) has just lost *all claim* on your life! Boaz had operated within the legal requirements and prevailed against the Law to acquire all that was Elimelech's, including Naomi and Ruth. Boaz owned it all!

I love this line: "to perpetuate the name of the dead." Aren't we those who were dead in our trespasses and sins? Aren't we now the ones who are being perpetuated through the redemptive acts of Christ? It is our name that *will not* be cut off from among the brethren. And the most amazing thing is that the Law is witness to all of it. There is absolutely no recourse, legal or ethical, to reverse this process. We are the Bride of Boaz, the prize of the GO'EL, the purchased, protected, cherished and restored object of the Redeemer's affection! Man, start celebrating!

> **4:11** | "And all the people who *were* at the gate, and the elders, said, '*We are* witnesses. The LORD make the woman who is coming to your house like Rachel and Leah, the two who built the house of Israel; and may you prosper in Ephrathah and be famous in Bethlehem.'"

Don't get so consumed in celebration that we lose sight of the fact that some real prophecy is taking place from here on out. It begins with the elders of the town wishing some specific blessings on Boaz.

MY NOTES

They wished for fame and prosperity in Bethlehem and prosperity in Ephrathah. So what does that last part mean? Well, it is important to understand a bit of genealogy here.

Caleb and Joshua were primarily in charge of the conquest of Canaan. Caleb settled in the new land and had some kids. One of those sons was "Hur," who was considered the father of Bethlehem. Hur's mother's name was Ephrathah. Since this Scripture dealt with wishes for Boaz's prosperity, but it is also related to his inclusion of Ruth, it was only fitting that these town elders referred to blessed women. One of the women they include is the mother to the father of Bethlehem. Let's hold that thought for a second.

Secondly, notice the town father's wish for Ruth. They hoped for her to be like Rachael and Leah. These two women represented the matriarchy of God's chosen nation, Israel. Isn't it interesting that Ruth became the representative of the Gentile nations becoming engrafted into the house of God. As Ruth said, "Your people *shall* be my people, And your God, my God" (Ruth 1:16).

Ruth would go on a be in the lineage of Christ. She would bear a child who represented the embracing of the child of promise into the Jewish nation. We'll see that part when we get to verse 16. For now, just notice that the town elders were wishing for the birth of a nation in the place from which Jesus would come. And they wished this before Micah had made his famous prophecy in Micah 5:2, that predicts the coming of Christ from Bethlehem. By the way, Micah mentions Ephrathah's name there, too.

MY NOTES

> **4:12** | "May your house be like the house of Perez, whom Tamar bore to Judah, because of the offspring which the LORD will give you from this young woman."

Again, the wish is for the prosperity of the line that will come from Bethlehem, Judah. Do you remember when we started this study? Elimelech came from Bethlehem, Judah. Now, the town fathers were praying for the prosperity that established the "house of bread" in the "place of praise" to continue in the house of Boaz. They had no idea how well God would answer this prayer for blessing. They simply couldn't know that the ultimate blessing—our Savior, Jesus Christ—would descend from this union.

From a genealogy standpoint, it's interesting that they would bring up Perez, Tamar, and Judah. The reason it's interesting is because of what is found in Judah's line of descendants. You see, Judah had five sons: Er, Onan, Shela, Perez, and Zerah. He arranged for a wife for his oldest son Er, and Genesis 38:6 tells us that the girl's name was Tamar. The problem was that Er and his brother Onan both died in the land of Canaan, leaving Shela as the only survivor. I know, you're wondering why there is only one son alive when we said that Judah had five sons. The last two sons hadn't been born yet. They were the fruit of a new marriage.

The bigger problem is that Er and Onan had both been married to a girl named Tamar. Judah was convinced that since both of them had died, Tamar must have had something to do with it. So, he refused to allow Shela to be a kinsman-redeemer and marry her. So, Judah took Tamar as his wife (acting as a kinsman-redeemer) through the Levirate Law, and Tamar gave birth to Perez and Zerah. From Perez came Hezron

MY NOTES

and Ram. And, if we look in the Matthew 1 account of Jesus's genealogy, those names lined up perfectly.

If we were to go into all the intricacies of this genealogical structure, it would be incredibly time-consuming. I suppose it's possible that most everyone would simply quit reading due to minutia and boredom. As a matter of fact, some of you may already be there—but I hope not. But before we move on, let me say this: Taking the time to research the intricate way that God included all the facets of redemption and Gentile inclusion into the process of Jesus's birth can leave any Bible student filled with amazement and gratitude! Don't think of it as a task. See it like a treasure hunt. You have been invited to go on a great adventure of discovery that will eradicate any doubt about *who* is eligible for salvation. The treasure available to everyone who takes the time to look is a discovery that God wants *all* of humanity to be saved (1 Timothy 2:4), and He's gone to extravagant lengths to demonstrate that truth. The most wonderful thing about this adventure is that along the way, there are an infinite number of discoveries to be acquired that were never the object of the initial pursuit. It's just a bonus on top of the original adventure. So, grab some books and start reading. If you'll remember, the very first words of the introduction of this little "notes" book admitted that there are volumes of commentary written by countless theologians that can help you discover the mysteries of Scripture. So, get going! Start your own adventure! There is treasure to be discovered if you hunt for it! It's promised.

> **4:13** | "So Boaz took Ruth and she became his wife; and when he went in to her, the LORD gave her conception, and she bore a son."

Pay close attention! You will not see Ruth's name mentioned again in this story. She is about to "fulfill her destiny." We see Ruth giving birth to the lineage that would produce our Messiah—who would give birth to the Church. We will see one more reference to her in a couple of verses, but her name then disappears. We'll have some discussion at the end of this chapter about the significance of this. But for now, just make note of it.

One other small thing: Notice that Ruth becomes the bride of Boaz (who is our type for Christ), and the bride continues the bloodline of Boaz by giving birth to a son. The life of Boaz is passed through Ruth just like the life-giving gospel is passed through the Church to those who would believe. Cyprian of Carthage goes as far as to say that, "You cannot have God for your Father and not have the Church for your mother." It's not Scripture, but it's a beautiful concept that is born out of truth.

What a beautiful picture of the life of Christ being passed through the Church to those who would become the children of God, servants of the Master, and the Bride of Christ. Boaz (a type for Jesus) is passing his life through Ruth (a type for the Church) to see his life-giving bloodline continue on to all who would become children of the King.

> **4:14-15** | "Then the women said to Naomi, 'Blessed *be* the LORD, who has not left you this day without a close relative; and may his name be famous in Israel! And may he be to you a restorer of life and a nourisher of your old age; for your daughter-in-law, who loves you, who is better to you than seven sons, has borne him.'"

We have spent so much time reading about the "close relative" and the "kinsman-redeemer" (GO'EL) that you will probably just assume

MY NOTES

that the women were talking about Boaz here. As a matter of fact, I've read respected commentaries that say exactly that. I'm never going to say that a commentator who is much smarter and more educated than me is wrong. There is definitely a way you can read this to infer that the statement is, at least in part, about Boaz. But you need to pay close attention to the way this blessing pans out. The whole thing ended with: "For your daughter-in-law . . . has *borne him.*" Ruth *did not* give birth to Boaz. Boaz gave birth *through* Ruth to their son, Obed. This entire speech was about the child that had been born to Ruth and Boaz. But Ruth was not in the speech. She was referred to as the daughter-in-law that bore the son, but her name is absent. This is a group of women who were speaking directly to Naomi. Where is Ruth? Isn't she the proud mama? Why aren't they singing a song to Ruth saying, "Blessed are you among women for God has granted to you a son?"

Well, let's go back to the start of verse 14 and review what's really going on here. The women started by saying that Naomi was blessed because she had received a close relative. But we already knew that they were not talking about Boaz; they were talking about the child. Then they say, "May *his* name be famous in Israel." This is a prophetic statement about what will come when the original people of God's covenant, Israel, accept Jesus the Christ as the true and living Son of God—which will happen, but that's another study. They wish that he would be a "restorer of life." Jesus is exactly that. They wish that he be a "nourisher of your old age." So, what does that one mean?

In Romans 11, God speaks of all of Israel being saved. I'm not going to begin to get into a large eschatological discussion about the cutting off of the Jewish branch in order to make room for the Gentile church. I'm not going to discuss what it means that the Church on earth is

MY NOTES

"caught up" when the fullness of the Gentiles is come in. I'm not going to defend the revelation of Christ to the Jewish people after the collecting of the Gentiles who have believed, or the "re-engrafting" of the Jewish branch into the vine of Christ. I'll let Scripture do all that for itself. Read Romans 11 closely and find the answers for yourself. Why don't you go collect your notes on all that material and share them with me? I'd love to read what you think.

I'll only say this: Naomi traveled away from her land and her people to encounter Ruth, a Gentile. This Gentile came into a relationship with God because she discovered His existence through the Jewish people. The Jews introduced the Gentiles to God. However, the Gentiles, along with the believing Jews, are those who ultimately embrace the Child of Bethlehem and become the Bride of Christ. At the end of our story, we see the Gentile (Ruth) handing the child who restores life and provides nourishment in the old age (of Judaism) back to Naomi (the Jews). Ruth disappeared from the story and Naomi was left with her people to extol the beauty and wonder of the child. That's not a difficult picture to see, is it?

> **4:16 |** "Then Naomi took the child and laid him on her bosom, and became a nurse to him."

Listen carefully. We began this story with an exclamation from Naomi, saying she was too old to give birth. She declared that even if she were able to conceive that her child would be insufficient for the needs of her daughters-in-law. So, the question begs, "How does Naomi now find the ability to 'nurse' the child?"

Our story is drawing to a close with a picture of the precious child—the restorer of life and nourisher—in the arms of the beloved Naomi,

MY NOTES

who had declared her repentance to God's lordship in her life. Ruth is gone from our story, and life flourishes between the child and the Jew. The Jews introduce Gentiles to God, and Gentiles re-introduce Christ, who is life, to the Jews. But it is God who restores fruitfulness to the bosom of Naomi and gave her the ability to offer life to the newly born in this family of redemption and faith.

> **4:17** | "Also the neighbor women gave him a name, saying, 'There is a son born to Naomi.' And they called his name Obed. He *is* the father of Jesse, the father of David."

If you have doubt about the nature or purpose of this birth, just look at this closing verse. There is no recordation in all of Scripture that Ruth gave birth to any other children. Ruth was the bride of Boaz, and she was honored as such in Matthew's genealogy of Jesus (Matthew 1:5). However, the fruit of that wedded union was passed back to Naomi in the form of a child who became the "close relative" for all of mankind—first for the Jew and then for the Gentile (Romans 1:16). Boaz was the kinsman-redeemer. He was the GO'EL. He is a type for Jesus Christ. Jesus, the restorer of life to the Jew. Jesus, the nourisher in the old age of God's chosen people. I know that this whole conclusion gets a little interwoven, but isn't the matter of redemption and life supposed to be a mystery—a mystery that is now revealed? It's a beautifully intricate and eternally wonderful picture of how Jew and Gentile, parent and child, are woven together to become the object of love and the inseparable family of God.

> **4:18-22** | "Now this *is* the genealogy of Perez: Perez begot Hezron; Hezron begot Ram, and Ram begot Amminadab;

MY NOTES

> Amminadab begot Nahshon, and Nahshon begot Salmon; Salmon begot Boaz, and Boaz begot Obed; Obed begot Jesse, and Jesse begot David."

Finally, our friend Samuel defends the place of David in the line of Christ and the ascension to the throne of Israel. Here, the historical and the prophetic come together into one statement. By defending the lineage of David, Samuel establishes the lineage of the Christ. May God bless us all—Jew and Gentile, male and female, young and old alike. May we find our place in Christ where the lines of separation are done away with, and the love of Christ makes us all one in a shared promise from an eternally loving God. Just as the Holy Spirit promised through Paul in Ephesians: "But now in Christ Jesus you who once were far off have been brought near by the blood of Christ. For He Himself is our peace, who has made both one, and has broken down the middle wall of separation, having abolished in His flesh the enmity, *that is*, the law of commandments *contained* in ordinances, so as to create in Himself one new man *from* the two, *thus* making peace, and that He might reconcile them both to God in one body through the cross, thereby putting to death the enmity" (Ephesians 2:13-16).

Chapter 4 Review

Chapter 4 is a picture of the gospel in action. It brings to mind Paul's declaration in Romans 3:26, "That He (God) might be just and the justifier of the one who has faith in Jesus." Boaz was going to expose the inability held in the Law, while simultaneously being completely obedient to it. As you work through the questions that follow, think of how this picture can help solidify your admiration for our Savior and how you can share the power of His saving love with someone who needs to know Him more fully.

1. Chapter 4 opens at what specific location? _____

2. What is the significance of the location mentioned in question 1? What typically happens there? _____

3. Boaz invited someone to sit down with him. What name did Boaz use to refer to the individual that he invited to sit with him? _____

4. Regarding family relationships, who was the man that Boaz invited to sit with him? _____

RUTH 4 REVIEW

5. What did the men discuss in questions 3 and 4 that represents the larger story of redemption? _____
_____

6. After the two of them are seated, Boaz invited _____ (how many) men to sit with them.

7. Why is the number in question 6 important? _____
_____
_____

8. Why is it important to pay attention to the name that Boaz used is question 3? _____
_____
_____

9. In verse 3, Boaz said that Naomi sold something. What did she sell? _____
_____

10. In verse 4, Boaz made a suggestion to the man seated next to him. What suggestion did he make? _____
_____
_____

11. What was the man's original response to the suggestion that Boaz made in verse 4? _____
_____
_____

12. In verse 5, Boaz included a caveat in his discussion. What caveat did he include? _____
_____

13. How did this alter the man's original response and why? _____
_____
_____
_____

14. In verse 7, what was the custom to confirm any matter of redeeming or exchanging anything? _____
_____
_____
_____

15. Deuteronomy 25:9 draws a very different picture of the redeeming/exchanging process. How is the passage in Deuteronomy different from the custom listed in verse 7? _____
_____
_____
_____

16. Why was Boaz able to do what the closer relative couldn't do? ___
_____
_____

17. In verse 11, the people of the city exclaimed, "The LORD make the woman who is coming to your house like Rachel and Leah." Who are Rachel and Leah and why is this exclamation important to our story? _____

_____

_____

18. In verse 14, the women of the town said to Naomi, "Blessed *be* the LORD, who has not left you this day without a *close relative* (redeemer)." Who is the "GO'EL" or "close relative" or "kinsman-redeemer" that the women were talking about? _____

_____

19. What was the name of the child born to Naomi (through Boaz and Ruth) and who would his grandson be? _____ and

_____

20. If you were to sum up this book in a handful of sentences, what would you say? _____

_____

_____

_____

_____

_____

_____

21. If you told someone you had just studied the Book of Ruth and they asked you what it was about, how would you answer? Remember, this might be your opportunity to invite someone into a deeper and fuller relationship with Jesus. So, don't just think of how you would convey the facts of the study. How would you convey the heart of the Jesus represented in the love of Boaz toward Ruth? How can you let your discussion of this book spread hope and happiness to the hearts of those you share it with? _____

_____

_____

_____

_____

_____

_____

_____

_____

_____

Let's Connect

Narrow Gate is a place where young men can quiet the distractions of everyday life and discover a life that matters, but it's also a community where people of all ages find purpose in supporting the mission of the organization.

Consider this your invitation to be a part of our family. Whether you're a young man who is considering becoming a student or a friend or family member who knows someone who would benefit from this experience, we invite you to:

- Follow us on Instagram @narrowgatelodge
- Follow us on Facebook @narrowgatefoundation
- Subscribe to our YouTube channel at Narrow Gate Foundation
- Shop our goods made for life at narrowgateleather.org
- Purchase our specialty fresh roast at narrowgate.coffee
- Help transform lives by transforming your home with our real wood beams, mantels, floating shelves and more at tnboxbeams.com
- Sign up for our email newsletters, request a Narrow Gate speaker, schedule a tour, or connect with our staff at info@narrowgate.org or 931-583-0633.

The eight-month residential experience at Narrow Gate Lodge is available to qualified young men, regardless of their financial resources. We have been able to offer students tuition-free experiences since our inception because of the generosity of thousands of people—and we invite you to join us. Narrow Gate is a 501(c)(3) nonprofit and donations are tax deductible.

Would you or your organization like to make a contribution or receive additional information?

Please contact us at:

931-583-0633

office@narrowgate.org

P.O. Box 267, Duck River, TN 38454

Are you a young man between the ages of 18 and 25 who would like to apply?

Learn more at:

nglodge.org